PRAISE FOR
Legacy List

Katie Parsons writes with such self-awareness and heart, guiding her readers back to their own values and purpose. *Legacy List* is a book for anyone who wants to leave the world even slightly better than they found it.

Virginia Walden Ford
Advocate and Subject of the 2019 movie *Miss Virginia*

Katie Parsons writes with an honesty that pulls you in as a reader. Her writing is conversational and warm even when she's tackling difficult subjects. As a writer, she speaks to you not at you, bringing curiosity and authenticity into her work. Readers will find her to be someone whose insights they can trust.

Mara Bellaby,
Executive Editor at *Florida Today*

Legacy List

how to create a life
that will outlive you

LEGACY LIST

Katie Parsons

Published and distributed by:
SOUND WISDOM
P.O. Box 310
Shippensburg, PA 17257-0310

717-530-2122

info@soundwisdom.com

www.soundwisdom.com

While efforts have been made to verify information contained in this publication, neither the author nor the publisher assumes any responsibility for errors, inaccuracies, or omissions. While this publication is chock-full of useful, practical information; it is not intended to be legal or accounting advice. All readers are advised to seek competent lawyers and accountants to follow laws and regulations that may apply to specific situations. The reader of this publication assumes responsibility for the use of the information. The author and publisher assume no responsibility or liability whatsoever on the behalf of the reader of this publication.

ISBN 13 TP: 978-1-64095-718-3

ISBN 13 eBook: 978-1-64095-719-0

For Worldwide Distribution, Printed in the U.S.A.

1 2 3 4 5 6 7 8 / 30 29 28 27 26

This book is dedicated to my mom,
who continues to give me the
right words when I need them.

CONTENTS

Prologue

WHAT IS A LEGACY?

"What is a legacy? It's planting seeds in a garden you never get to see."

—Lin-Manuel Miranda

Have you ever had a moment when your entire being came suddenly into focus? That moment when, like a thick bolt of lightning against a dark sky, you see so clearly—if for a brief moment—your intended path?

I've had a handful of moments like this in my four-plus decades of life. There was the time I saw my first Broadway touring show at age 10, nestled between my parents at the Chicago Theatre, watching the ridiculous talent of the performers and technicians in the classic *Showboat.* I wanted to be up on stage too and every step I took from that day forward was one to get me closer.

There was the time at age 16 when I was driving through the beginning of a snowstorm, and I lost control of my vehicle on a highway, spinning into oncoming traffic and nearly missing a direct hit by a motorist trying desperately to brake. I vowed to never take a moment of safety for granted (spoiler: I have taken many moments since for granted) and to just generally be more observant.

And then there was that moment, exhausted and alone, when I held my first baby in my arms at age 25 and everything I'd ever done up until that point paled in comparison to the responsibility I instantly felt. I promised to make the world better for her, starting in our home.

I think we've all had these revelations: those moments when the sheer potential of that second in time overwhelms and changes us forever. Sometimes these are moments of joy and pure connection. Other times these are moments of panic or trauma that shape us for the path forward.

After years of deeply examining my own life and purpose, I've come to realize that these moments are core components of our legacies—of what we are called to build upon before our time here on Earth ends. These moments, when viewed through a lens of our callings, have the potential to reverberate for decades, or even centuries, after we've left our humble homes here.

Perhaps my biggest moment of sudden, extreme life focus happened when I was 37 years old and my mother was diagnosed with early-onset Alzheimer's disease at the age of 64. Suddenly I was calling into question everything that I'd ever done with my own life. Had I made enough memories with her? Was I making enough memories with my own kids? When would she stop remembering who I was? How much time did I still have with a sound mind? What did I still need to accomplish?

Like most loved ones of dementia patients, the diagnosis was a long time coming. For several years the symptoms had existed but were written off, by all of us, as "something else." For most of those years, we attributed the changes to other factors like stress, hormones, and even her general quirkiness. She was too young and healthy to be experiencing dementia—it *had* to be something else.

But as quirkiness gave way to confusion, it was clearly time for my dad, my brothers, and I to face the music. That's why on January 1, 2019, I found myself sitting alone in a middle seat on a discount flight from Orlando to Chicago to visit my parents, who lived just over the Indiana line on the south shore of Lake Michigan. As I played a silent game of "whose armrest is this anyway?" with the passengers to my right and left, I closed my eyes and felt the invisible weight of what I was literally flying toward settle on my chest.

I remember feeling extreme dread during that flight—not because I disliked flying, but because I knew what was waiting for me when I touched down in snowy, icy Chicago. The good part, a hug from my dad, and the grueling part, several appointments with neurologists and other practitioners with my mom during the visit. But this was a trip I asked for that included components I wanted to experience firsthand, a firstborn personality trait.

And the trip kicked off a three-month litany of referrals and appointments that landed me back in Indiana in March to meet with a neurologist. The findings were clear. Mom was struggling with Alzheimer's disease. Dad and I tried to take in the details that day, as Mom sat silent. When we got to the car, she started to cry. From the passenger's backseat, I leaned forward to put my arm on her shoulder and said, "It's okay, Mom. Now we can try to help you."

As the reality of her diagnosis set in, though, I wondered if it really was going to be okay. Day by day, my own anxiety rose. I felt grief for what was already lost and what I knew would be lost moving forward. But it was more than just grief that I felt.

Like that bolt of lightning across a black sky, I felt a jolt of urgency inside me that had never been as strong. I wanted to do all the things my heart desired—immediately. Maybe I didn't have as much time as I thought I did. Maybe my body would make it to my golden years, but what about my brain?

Back home, I started to resent my day-to-day routine, from my morning runs to the editing work I was doing for a newsletter publisher. Every room of my house started to close in on me with all of its flaws magnified, another reminder of all I wasn't getting done. Time with my five children felt heavy, as I thought of all the places we hadn't yet visited, and all the things I hadn't made happen yet as their parent. I started to feel overwhelmed by the weight of all I hadn't yet done.

The revelation that time, and specifically cognitive time, is finite had never been so clear to me.

As I felt my own reality spiraling, I realized that in order to address the urgency building within me, I needed a plan, an outline, a blueprint. I needed a way to organize the thoughts in my brain and make them make sense before they fully consumed me.

So I started a process of questioning, auditing, writing, and editing that I now refer to as my *Legacy List*. This months-long endeavor included auditing my schedule, prioritizing commitments, crossing obligations right off the list, and nailing down my true "why" in life. I did all of this from the perspective of what I believed in my heart of hearts was my true calling in this life—the thing only I can set in motion that will outlive me. The thing that will make a difference in my life, my children's lives, and the world long term.

And that thing may not be flashy or look materialistically huge on paper. I may never be famous, or wealthy, or a best-selling author (thank you for buying this book, by the way). My legacy may be the smallest ripple in the universe that improves someone's life or direction, or makes the world just slightly better. But my legacy will have the biggest impact if I'm consciously aligned.

And that is the whole reason I'm here right now, retracing my steps to help you create your own Legacy List.

Time is finite but our potential is not.

Introduction

YOUR STARTING POINT

Have you ever stopped to think about your existence? I don't mean the space you occupy at this very moment in time. Have you ever really taken the time to consider how every moment had to connect to the next to bring you to where you are today? It's a bit overwhelming if you start to stack up all of the moments in time that had to align perfectly for you to be exactly here, right now.

Psychologists have long studied the connection between purpose and well-being. One of the most influential figures in this field, Viktor Frankl, wrote in *Man's Search for Meaning*[1] that having a clear sense of purpose is essential to human survival and happiness. His research found that individuals who believe their lives have meaning tend to be more resilient, even in the face of extreme adversity.

1. Viktor Frankl, *Man's Search for Meaning* (Beacon Press, 2006. Originally published 1946).

A study published in *The Journal of Positive Psychology* found that individuals with a strong sense of purpose are more likely to engage in meaningful work and report higher job satisfaction.[2] Another study conducted at the University of Michigan revealed that people with a strong sense of purpose tend to live longer, healthier lives.[3]

But what does having "a calling" or "living with purpose" even really mean? Finding the crux of that meaning centers on a concept called a "flow state," introduced by psychologist Mihaly Csikszentmihalyi.[4]

A flow state occurs when a person is fully immersed in an activity that challenges their skills but is deeply enjoyable. In this state, time seems to disappear, and productivity skyrockets. Research has found that individuals who frequently enter a flow state are not

---

2. Kinga Mnich, PhD, "What Is Job Satisfaction and Why Is It Important?" *PositivePsychology.com,* May 14, 2025. https://positivepsychology.com/job-satisfaction/.

3. Vic Strecher, "The power of purpose: How our deepest intentions shape our health," *Pursuit,* April 18, 2024, University of Michigan School of Public Health; https://sph.umich.edu/pursuit/2024posts/the-power-of-purpose-how-our-deepest-intentions-shape-our-health.html.

4. Sarah Steimer, "Mihaly Csikszentmihalyi, pioneering psychologist and 'father of flow,' 1934-2021," *UChicagoNews,* October 28, 2021; https://news.uchicago.edu/story/mihaly-csikszentmihalyi-pioneering-psychologist-and-father-flow-1934-2021; accessed November 1, 2025.

only happier but also perform at higher levels in their respective fields.

Thankfully, flow isn't sequestered to what you do for a paycheck. In fact, in many cases the opposite is true, with flow being found in activities that don't usually align with a paid job.

The things we do when we experience that flow state give our lives that extra bit of oomph, or purpose. We often feel rejuvenated, and then completely drained, when we tap into our flow activities. They give us a boost that tells us in the back of our mind: *Hey, this feels good. Do more of it.*

Flow moments aren't designed just to make us feel good, though. There is inherent value in doing things that are just fun, or feel fulfilling, of course. But if we can learn to take the cues from those flow moments, we can start to piece together a life that feels both meaningful and satisfying.

This book is designed to help you identify those flow moments, alongside your values and goals, and to begin to understand your sacred responsibility to yourself and your fellow humans to notice how those things align with your calling in this life—and to act on them.

Bucket List Versus Legacy List

You've probably heard the term "bucket list" before. A bucket list contains experiences, goals, or achievements a person wants to accomplish during their lifetime. It can include anything from adventurous activities (such as skydiving or traveling to a specific country) to personal milestones (such as writing a book, running a marathon, or learning any new skill). The idea is to intentionally pursue meaningful or exciting things before life runs out.

It's an exciting concept, though the actual term *bucket list* is a bit morbid in origin. It comes from the phrase "kick the bucket," which is a colloquial way of saying "to die." I won't weigh you down with the gory details of why that term was coined but I will say that it does date back to 18th century farming.

The phrase *bucket list* itself was popularized in modern culture by the 2007 film *The Bucket List* starring Jack Nicholson and Morgan Freeman. In the movie, two terminally ill men make a list of things they want to do before they "kick the bucket" and set out to complete them. After the movie's release, the term quickly entered mainstream use.

The exercise of writing a bucket list tells us a lot about who we are as people and reveals our inner wishes. It can also reveal a lot about our values, based on what we want to do and who we want beside us. Taking the steps to complete items on a bucket list has the potential to enhance the human experience, making us wiser, kinder, and more aware of what our lives mean in the bigger picture.

It's also just fun to make a bucket list, right? It's always a good time to sit down with a coffee, or your beverage of choice, and to imagine the possibilities within our one precious lifetime on this absolutely amazing planet with so much to offer us.

There's an expiration date on a bucket list, though. Its name and meaning reference the inevitability of death. It's a frank reminder that whether we dream big and chase those dreams hard, or just meander through life, the end of it eventually comes.

A bucket list requires completion by the end of a person's life, which, by the way, is not something anyone knows for certain. This list relies heavily on the human experience for the person living it, drawing on the actions that person wants to take before they leave this world, or "kick the bucket."

But what happens after that? What happens when someone inevitably reaches their demise and all that's left are the unfinished desires on that bucket list? Based on what items were purposefully completed, maybe some of the bucket list items reverberate. Maybe some leave a lasting impact. It's true that every action we take creates ripples, perhaps even after we are gone.

But the basis of creating and following through on a bucket list is that it has a finite term. It's meant to satisfy the person experiencing it with what the world has to offer. Meaningful experiences can stem from the actions of that list, but it's designed to fulfill the wants of the person checking off said dreams.

So, I ask again, what happens after that?

Let me rephrase that: What if there was a more purposeful way to plan for this life—and the life that will continue when we are gone? What if the experiences we strive for in this life are rooted in longer-term alignment? Can we create a life that reverberates well beyond our expiration date?

That's where a Legacy List comes in.

I often think of my great-grandparents when the topic of legacy arises. I imagine what questions they might have about modern life and how people live now—more than 120 years since they were born, and 50 years since they've died. In their wildest dreams, would they have ever conceived of the internet or personal cell phones or streaming TV?

Could they have imagined as Polish immigrants, crammed below the deck of a hot, damp boat that their great-granddaughter would be sitting at her Florida dining room table midday, listening to the dryer toss her pool towels to get them fluffy, sipping an extra coffee, and typing away on a book about the legacies that we leave?

The purposeful actions they took when they left Poland to start a new legacy in the United States of America are the reason I'm here right now, doing just that. If they had done anything differently, I'd cease to exist and so would my children. And so would a lot of other people. And yet, people are always making decisions that determine the next part of their stories, and what will be told about them in future generations. We don't have the insight to see the "what ifs" that could have been alternative paths. We only have what resulted from the actual actions that were taken.

And when I view legacy in that way, I am humbled. One change of heart about moving across the world, and my genetic companions would still be on a hillside somewhere in Poland (I imagine Poland has a lot of grassy hillsides, but I've never been there. It's on my bucket list to visit). I wouldn't be here and you wouldn't be reading these words right now, maybe with a cup of coffee or glass of wine, listening to the hum of your home appliances around you.

But I am here. And you are too (thank you, by the way). We're here because of a series of decisions that led to the point of our conception and birth. And we are together in this book because we both know what a gift this life is, especially when we consider the "what if" alternatives. We're here because we know we need to make that count for something, beyond our bucket lists.

Why a Legacy List, though? Like, what does that even mean? Is it financial or spiritual or familial or career-based? Yes. It is all of those things, and more. Your Legacy List applies to every part of your being that tugs at you and makes you feel empowered and alive. It is about all of the wildly wonderful components of your personality, values, and experiences that really do matter in this world.

The Legacy List that you create by the end of this book will enable you to create that life that will outlive you. How that manifests will be as unique as each person reading this book—but the way we arrive at that point will be a collective exercise in finding the crux of our calling, and the actions it will take to root it in our life and the lives we will affect now, and for long into the future.

The following is what you need to get the most out of this book:

1. A place to jot down your thoughts, and complete the exercises in the book. Keep that place handy as you move through this book. You can use

physical paper or a notebook, or opt for a digital notebook. This can be a running document on your computer, your Notes app, or anywhere you can revisit these answers later. I keep all of my journal questions and answers in a single notebook, using colorful pens to delineate my answers. When I fill a notebook, I simply buy another one and keep them all together. I know plenty of people who successfully write and journal electronically, though. As long as you keep all of your thoughts organized in a single space for the duration of the exercises in this book, you will get the most out of them. It also makes it easier to reference later on, or compare down the road if you revisit any of the exercises.

2. Privacy so that you feel open enough to read and complete the exercises in this book honestly. Evaluate your life and write openly, as if no one in the world will ever see what you write. If you choose to share some of your thoughts later on, that is your choice. But write as if you are the only one who will ever read it.

3. Time to dedicate to each exercise. Building your Legacy List is a step-by-step process and each exercise is built on the one before it. If you are

> on a reading tear, and you want to just keep reading and not stop for the exercises, that's perfectly fine. But be sure not to skip any of the exercises in order when you do loop back to complete them.

By the end of this book, you should have an actionable path that helps you set up your Legacy List for the future. Some pages will be harder to process than others; and some answers will be easier to find than others. Remember that there are no wrong paths. Every answer is going to be custom to the individual jotting it down. Perfection is not the goal; alignment is. You will read a lot about my Legacy List process and the life I've lived up to this point. I hope that my own journey in progress can help you feel more fulfilled in yours.

I'm honored to help you create your Legacy List, with dreams and hopes and ripples that far outlive you. So without further ado, let's get started.

1

WHO ARE YOU, ANYWAY?

Around the age of 11, just when my pre-teen hormonal development was starting to ramp up, I developed an interesting way to freak myself out royally. I'd look at my reflection in the mirror—all of my gangly, frizzy-haired and gap-toothed self—and ask myself this question aloud: "Who are you, anyway?"

It sounds pretty straightforward, right? The human experience is in fact asking questions about ourselves and our world over and over again in the search for meaning, and then adding things to our lives to make us more fully ourselves (for better or for worse). It wasn't the question that really made the hair stand up on my neck, though. It was the direct way I asked it, looking myself in the eye. In an instant I'd feel disconnected from the person looking back at me. It was almost as if that reflection was a different entity—a person created to look a certain way without my consent, whose fashion choices and mannerisms were products of her environment. Heck, even the way I sounded asking the question felt like it was coming from a foreign body.

Staring back at myself, the true person looking back at me, I would quickly feel overwhelmed thinking about my identity and how it aligned with the person I saw and heard. So, I'd shake off those goose bumps, put some gel in my permed hair and pack up my homework for school.

Eventually the urge to analyze the soul behind that appearance faded. As I got closer to adulthood, I was so busy with the act of living that I didn't have the time or desire to examine my inner self and outer presentation too closely. One activity led to another, relationships came and went, my body shot up to its final height at 5' 7" and according to nature and the law, I grew up. That soul beneath my youthful exterior became harder to find, pushed further down by each life choice followed by another.

It wasn't until I was in my late 30s that I revisited that mirror-facing question from my youth. I looked at myself in the mirror of my bathroom, squaring my shoulders to really look at my reflection, and asked aloud:

"Who are you, anyway?"

I felt the familiar chills of my middle-school years flood my body. I was asking the same person the same question, only this version of that person was even further from an answer than she'd been at age 11. Instead of feeling overwhelmed at the possibilities of who I could one day become, I felt crushed by the weight of the actual person who had transpired. Years later and I still wasn't sure how to answer this one simple question about myself.

It wasn't that anything was specifically wrong in my life or with the person in that reflection. I wasn't a bad person. I was a good mother. I was a messy, but otherwise loyal and attentive, wife and partner. I cared deeply for my friends, my neighbors, my community, and animals. My daily interactions with the world were positive, and I felt like I left most places better than when I found them (unless it was my bathroom, where the counter bent under the weight of all of my face creams, hair ties, and discarded coffee mugs).

There was nothing really wrong with the person looking back at me. She was acceptable by most measures of a person, and above average in others. I didn't hate her. But I just had this overwhelming feeling that I didn't actually *know* her. Like, at all. Who was this woman who at age 11 had wondered about what life would look like at this age and stage? I really wasn't sure if all of the layers of my life really represented the core of me, the soul of who I am. The stranger looking back at me freaked me out.

But worse than that was the overwhelming feeling that the real me was not actually lost. She was in there, somewhere. The answer to my question was buried under the layers of life I'd piled on. The woman looking back at me in the mirror seemed distant from the core of who I really was—but how far down would I have to dig to find her?

It didn't help that I was in the throes of an existential crisis stemming from my mom's Alzheimer's disease diagnosis. I didn't know how much time I truly had to dig deep and find myself. Who was I at my core? Would I ever find out? The weight and possibility of those questions stuck with me in the weeks that followed.

As I thought more about the "who" of myself, I realized that there was a dichotomy forming. There was the "who" of me in real life, at that moment. And the "who" that I felt I wanted to be, or was just scratching the surface of in my everyday life. I knew I couldn't get to the bottom of who I was until I addressed both of these beings: the actual "who" and the ideal "who."

I had never really stopped to examine my life in such a holistic way. Most of the things that filled my day were things I had said "yes" to in a vacuum: my job, my marriage, my children, the cars sitting in my driveway and the house I lived in and their maintenance, the volunteer commitments, my friendships, and even social events on my calendar. They had all entered the timeline of my life separately—as individual entities that contributed to the whole. At one time, each individual thing made sense to include in my life—and some items had a more permanent position in the makeup of my life, like being a spouse and mother.

But what about everything else? What about the commitments that were not necessarily lifelong ones? How many were there? How did they get there? Did the "yes" that I at one time gave them still make sense?

So I got out a piece of paper and started to ask myself some of the tough questions I knew I needed to answer to really address the person inside—and from there, the person I wanted to become. I've since revisited this exercise and added some nuance to the original questions. I find myself drawn back to this specific exercise when I'm in moments of indecision, or even turmoil. Anytime I feel uncertain about my "who," I look at my past answers, and answer the questions anew. These moments of reflection are often enough to put my finger on the heart of the problem and find my way back to the soul underneath.

What follows is a guided exercise for you to start answering some of these soul-searching questions yourself. Try not to feel overwhelmed at the limitations as you write this out—we will work through those obstacles as we continue to encounter more exercises in this book. Give yourself permission to be honest and get to the bottom of who you really are, anyway.

Exercise: Getting to the Core of You

We spend a lot of time getting to know the people in our lives, from our romantic partners to our coworkers or kids' teachers. Societally we've developed pathways to get to know people, at least on a surface level. From small talk in person, to scrolling through their social media to see what causes they champion, how they spend their Saturdays, and what they eat for lunch. This is a reciprocal task, of course. Just as we are getting to know the people in our lives, they are getting to know us. And in both cases, the person who is "getting to know" the other can only learn as deeply as their subject allows. We never truly know who we are meeting, even if they end up as part of our lives for years to come.

We wear a lot of masks for others—and most are not nefarious, but are simply us controlling the narrative about ourselves for the rest of the world. But what happens when we get so accustomed to that mask that we start to believe it ourselves? What happens when we stop getting to know ourselves, and start accepting the "us" that we simply present? It's easier to just accept who we are at face value than to do that deeper work to discover who we truly are or who we truly want to be. But that's the easy way out. That's the shortcut to being comfortable in a life that should actually be full of challenges. We can do better than that—and really should.

The following questions are designed to tap into the "you" of right now, and the "you" who is hiding. These answers are meant to make you reflect, and to question the real you who is struggling to emerge from the clutter of life. Give yourself permission to be honest in what you answer. You will likely find at least remnants of the person you want to be—and that's where we start our Legacy List journey.

Time to Write It Down

1. Write a brief biography about yourself from the perspective of someone who knows you well. This can be a partner, a friend, a colleague, or anyone who knows you about as well as a person can. What would they say in your bio if they wrote it? This can be as surface level or as descriptive as you'd like. If you think people in different spheres of your life would right it differently, then write a few of them. Example: Katie Parsons is a writer who likes to

tell her own real-life stories. She is a mom of five and loves animals. She gets up early every day and enjoys tasty coffee. Katie loves to travel and sing.

2. Now write your own bio, based on your life right now, including your age. Include what you do for work, family, and fun. This should be a matter-of-fact assessment and to the point of who you are right now.

3. Write a bio about the "you" that will exist in five years, including that updated age. Include any goals you aim to accomplish, any major changes in your life, and anything from the other bios that are still relevant.

4. Now write down five words that describe you *today,* and put today's date. These can be positive words such as driven, motivated, kind, or struggle-based, scattered, unenergized, lost. Try to find the five words that truly encapsulate who you are as you write these down. If you feel limited by only having access to five words, try writing down as many as you want and then going back through and circling the top five.

5. Write down the five words you hope describe you five years from now, and put that future

date. Some of the words may overlap between current you and future you, and that is okay. It just means that you are already on the right track. On the flip side, don't be discouraged if your current words are not a reflection of who you hope to be in five years. This is meant to be an honest assessment of where you are now, and where you hope to go.

6. Finally, imagine you are living your last day here on earth. There's no sadness or despair. You have done everything you wanted to do on both your bucket and legacy lists. Write out these accomplishments, and get as specific as you'd like. The following is a template to follow: I am (NAME) and I have lived a good life. I have set out to achieve (LIST) and have accomplished it. I am (DESCRIBE GOOD THINGS ABOUT YOURSELF). I am leaving behind a legacy of (WHAT IS THE LEGACY).

Keep this first exercise nearby as you continue reading the book.

2

WHAT DO YOU REALLY WANT TO DO?

When was the last time someone asked you this question: "What do you want to do?"

Maybe it was today, when you were making plans for the coming weekend with a friend or family member. Maybe it was at your last work meeting when discussing an upcoming project. Maybe you can't remember the last time anyone even asked for your input on what you want to do—and look, that's okay too.

The point is that along the way, someone has asked each of us this question, whether it was a well-meaning aunt or uncle asking us what we want to be when we grow up or our car mechanic asking if we want to opt for the high-priced repair or the lower-priced that will get us by for now.

People ask other people this question, in all languages and in all parts of the world. And really, it puts the person replying on the spot. It's a loaded question because it implies that our answer will determine the next step. That once we give a response, our words will set in motion what comes next, whether it is a Saturday night dinner reservation or middle-of-the-line brake pads for our car.

Being a decider sounds empowering, but it's also a big responsibility. It's a fork in the road asking us which way to go, or a series of numbered doors where we can only choose one to see what's hiding behind. Even if a choice on what we want to do seems obvious to us, there's a bit of doubt and anxiety that can creep into the decider's psyche. Particularly if the decision we make will affect other people or situations that are outside our own personal experience. We feel the responsibility of deciding what we want to do, especially if anyone else at all will be impacted by our answer to that question.

Imagine for a moment, though, that this question is being asked in a vacuum. There is truly no wrong answer and nothing will fail, and no one will be harmed or bothered based on your answer. Imagine it as an open-ended question that is about anything in the entire world. If there was no financial, physical, or emotional cost, answer this question:

What do you want to do?

Sit with it for a moment. If it seems too vast a question to find any answer, try answering it in your head on a small scale. What do you want to do in the next five minutes? What do you want to do by the end of today? What do you want to do this weekend, next month, next year?

What do you want to do by the end of your time here on earth?

As mentioned in this book's Introduction, people often refer to what they want to do in their life as a "bucket list." And let's face it, there are definitely a lot of wonderful things about living life as a human being on this planet that are admirable to want to experience, from travel to food to wine to family life. For all the grand, wonderful high-quality experiences we want to have, however, there is also the reality of day-to-day life. And making that daily routine as fulfilling and enjoyable as possible should really be our goal, shouldn't it? That's the real life we actually live, day in and day out.

This doesn't necessarily mean living a "happy" life day in and day out. Happy is a temporary state triggered by our surroundings or feelings. Anger and sadness are in the same vein. There's a difference between experiencing happiness and experiencing contentment, however.

Contentedness is a state of being that is stable, despite the outside forces around you. You may feel content in a relationship because you trust and admire that other person, even on the days when that person annoys you. You may feel content with your career path, even if the tasks of the job are tedious or feel empty at times. When you are aligned, even the "hard days" will seem less daunting, as you experience alignment with the path of your life.

When we think about the trajectory of our lives in terms of happiness versus contentment, we come to realize that there is truly no single perfect day. But we can work toward sustaining our contentment through aligning ourselves with our core values and goals.

Exercise: Designing Your Sustainable Day

If you woke up tomorrow and could spend your day doing *anything,* what would it be?

This cliche question is designed to help us get to the bottom of what our heart desires in life. I've always wrestled with this question, though.

Designing a perfect *single* day is different from designing a life that you wake up to over and over again—a life that is sustainable.

For example, if I crafted a single perfect day, it would probably include staying in my PJs, drinking a little extra coffee, catching up on time with my kids and husband, and finally binge-watching shows that were popular five years ago. Add in some time hugging my dogs and sitting at my piano and singing (still in my PJs) and *that* would be my perfect, singular day.

And as chill and comforting as that day sounds, it isn't the type of day I'd want to experience over and over again. For one thing, the day I described includes a lot of "catch up" things, like catching up on sleep, caffeine, hugs, family time, and TV shows. That day sounds wonderful to me now because my normal, average days don't allow time for those activities right now.

But when I think about the long-term trajectory of my life, I don't want small spurts of catching up. I want a sustainable life that holds both my dreams and my energy in balance, allowing me closeness to those people, places, and experiences that I love.

So instead of asking you, reader, what your perfect day would look like, I'll ask this: "What does a perfect day look like that you can repeat over and over again?"

You may wonder what this question actually has to do with getting to the true “you.” It’s simpler than it seems. The way we want to spend our time says a lot about our core selves. It helps us come to terms with the way we’d really like our world to operate. And that is a tangible way to discover just how close we truly are to the “who” inside.

Let’s put our pen to paper, or fingers to the keyboard or touchscreen. For this exercise, you will design a routine day in your future that you’d love to experience, over and over again. Use these questions to guide you—then write out your schedule, beginning with when you wake up to when you lay down at night.

Time to Write It Down

For each question, answer honestly what this looks like right now. Then in a parallel column or on the next line, write what you want your answer to be in an ideal situation.

1. What time do you wake up on a typical day? What is your ideal time that you like to wake up? For the sake of this question, remove any constraints like your job or your family’s schedule. Simply write what that ideal time would be for you if you were able to choose it.

2. What is the *first* thing you do when you wake up each day? What is the first thing you would want to do when you wake up?

3. What else is part of your morning routine, be as specific as possible. This should include everything you do before the "work" of your day starts, whether that is a full-time job, gig work, volunteer work, going to school, or handling domestic tasks. Now ask yourself: *What would my ideal morning routine look like?*

4. What does the work of your typical day look like? When does it start and what tasks are you completing? Take a few minutes to write out what you love about that work and what you dislike. Now, what would your daily "work" look like if you could choose it?

5. What else fills your non-work hours? What are your hobbies? What are your obligations? This should include anything at home or other family obligations. Which of those things would you keep in an ideal schedule, and which would you limit or eliminate?

6. Who do you interact with every day? This can include your daily people—family who lives in your home, your coworkers, your neighbors—

but you can also list the people you see at least weekly, depending on the day. This list should also include anyone you communicate with regularly from afar, either through texts, emails, or phone calls. Now of this list, who is missing? Who do you wish you had more time or energy to connect with on a daily or fairly regular schedule? And who do you wish you could interact with less? These may be people you don't currently interact with daily, for example a sibling or parent. List anyone you'd at least want to touch base with every day.

7. What are you doing that is just for fun? This could be reading, getting out in nature, enjoying a sport or hobby, or anything that just fills your proverbial amusement cup. When does it make the most sense for these things to happen?

8. What time do you want to go to bed at night? Are you naturally a night owl? Or do you prefer mornings? Or are you at your best in the middle of the day?

From these questions, create a timeline for a perfect day. Even if you find that nothing on your list matches your current day right now—make that list. From waking until sleep, what does your day look like? This doesn't mean you have to fill every moment with productivity or "doing" anything. In fact, there should be leisure and other downtime written in. It may take a perspective shift to view the time as yours, and not just opportunities to get things done. Write as if there is no standard for what you should do in a day, no limit to what you are allowed to do and when. From there, your perfect day will emerge.

Hold on to this list to use as we continue through the book.

3

IS THERE ROOM ON YOUR PLATE?

If there is one lesson I seem to have trouble learning over and over again in life it is this that when you add something to your proverbial plate, something else has to go. The amount of time in a day that you have—that *everyone* has—is concrete. Time does not expand to meet the demands of our lives. We have to fit our obligations into the small windows of time in our lives.

When you add something new, removing something else is the only way to balance it. But how many of us actually stop to think: *What will I need to **stop** doing to add this other thing?* And if you don't remove that thing—if it just stays there, dangling by a thread as the new demands of your life enter—it will eventually drop itself off the side of that plate, and often make quite a mess in the process.

This truly isn't finger-pointing, unless you count the finger pointing at me. New minutes do not magically add on to our hours because we'd like to fill those minutes with something new to do. And it's a lesson that I continue to work on. I kid you not. I once started a new full-time job without quitting my current one. The timing "wasn't right" in my mind to quit my current job. My boss was on leave, I had a few projects I wanted to wrap up before I left, etc.

Both were remote jobs, and in my mind I could just toggle between the two until I felt like my time to leave the afore-obtained job had arrived. Since a lot of my work was done independently, I didn't foresee a whole bunch of time conflicts. I did have some meetings though. Hmmm. I was going to just figure that out as I went, I guess.

And then there was the issue of actual time in the day to *do* all the independent work that would still need to be done at some point. 4 a.m.? Saturdays while sitting in the stands of my daughter's volleyball games? I hadn't really thought that part through yet.

I would've just barreled forward with this really ill-conceived plan, but thankfully, the universe intervened within the first five days of working at both places. For as big as the remote-work world is nowadays, it's sort of small too. Someone at my new job happened to message someone from my previous job about something totally unrelated—and mentioned that they were excited that I joined their team. The very confused person at my current (well, my old-current) job went and asked my supervisor about it, completely innocently thinking I had quit without their knowledge.

That boss asked me point blank if I had accepted a new job, and I admitted that I had. I explained my good intentions (surely that would earn me some ethics points) but it was too late. My email and instant messaging access was cut off immediately and I was sent a FedEx packing slip to return my company-issued laptop.

My boss couldn't believe how nonchalant I was about my plan to work two full-time jobs. Was I punking her? Was I serious? And I apologized for the error in my thought pattern, which was really pretty obvious as I stopped to think about it.

A Plate Too Full

This is an extreme example of just adding things to my plate without much forethought. I wish I could say this happened in my 20s, or even my 30s, but no. I was 41 years old, with 15-plus years in the professional workplace and five kids under my roof when I made this choice. Well into my Legacy List process. In my mind, two jobs would help me get ahead so that I could loop back to the things on my Legacy List and be able to afford them. But what I was missing in this thought pattern was the fact that money is not the only resource we cannot duplicate. Time is too.

In less metaphoric terms, our time and energy is finite. We cannot add more time to our days. We cannot create extra space in our homes and offices without rearranging what is already there. And as much as modern life tries to tell us differently, we cannot multitask endlessly into a productivity abyss. Even more simply put—we do not have enough time to do it all.

I've always been an "over-scheduler," even as a kid. I remember as a second grader taking out pieces of lined paper from my school composition notebooks and writing out what I'd be doing every minute of an upcoming Saturday. No minute was idle. If my time wasn't occupied with something structured, like gymnastics or swimming lessons, I filled every second with something else, like cuddle time with my stuffed animals or singing practice (music I'd written myself, of course). There was no downtime, at least none that wasn't documented. To feel accomplished, I felt as if each moment needed its own assignment.

What years of wisdom and professional therapy have helped me realize about little me is that overscheduling was, and still is, a form of control and escapism. It was (and is) my way of capturing time and compartmentalizing it so that I could feel in control. The act of planning is the escapism part. By sitting with a notebook and colorful pens, and color blocking the wishes I wanted to complete, I was escaping the actual moment I was in.

Now, don't get me wrong, squaring up my schedule and taking some time for reflection each week is a valuable part of how I organize my thoughts, remind myself of tasks I need to complete, and more. And a celebrated one. Too often we equate our worth with the number of things we can check off our to-do list, never stopping to analyze exactly what is on that list in the first place.

When I faced that existential, looking-in-the-mirror question in my late 30s, I knew that the bits and pieces of life that had come together as the mosaic of what I saw, and what I had come to represent.

I knew that to get to the core of the legacy I was truly supposed to leave behind, I needed to first audit what my actual schedule, responsibilities, and obligations looked like in real-time. I needed to audit my life. Not an idealized version of what my life was like (that comes later), but an actual accounting of what it looked like in my day-to-day. I needed to know where my precious time was going and assess it.

Looking at your schedule may seem like a no-brainer. Between digital calendars, phone reminders, emails confirming appointments, and even our own handwritten planners, our schedules may seem easily digestible, always in the forefront. But what I found when I carefully, thoughtfully, and neutrally deconstructed my responsibilities was this: I was no longer choosing this schedule. It had chosen me, over years of adding a half hour commitment here, or a monthly obligation there. When I added in the schedules of my family, and my own involvement there, it was even more jarring. What *were* all these things on my docket? And *why* were they all there?

The Audit

So I started an audit of what currently existed in my life. I took out a piece of plain, white computer paper and grabbed several colors of markers from my kitchen junk drawer. I gave each category of my life a color, and just started writing.

When I'd written out an entire week, I looked at what items existed outside of it. What commitments were biweekly or monthly or even more spaced out? I added those in the assigned colors to the sheet. For each item I wrote on my list, I wrote three time frames:

how much time it took per week, per month, and per year.

I walked away from the list and revisited it for about a week, adding new things as they came to my mind. As I went through my daily and weekly routine, I wrote down the commitments that didn't make it to the calendar—things like grocery shopping, calling to make appointments, cleaning my home, paying my bills—anything that I could think of that took time, but hadn't made it to my official calendar docket. The list got longer and longer as the days went by.

After I was pretty sure I'd written down nearly *everything* that made up my current life commitments, I was amazed at all it entailed, staring at me from a piece of computer paper in multicolored glory. Was I even sleeping? Second-grade me would have likely been impressed. But 37-year-old me felt discouraged. According to this handwritten accounting, there was no time for anything else.

But I also felt something positive creep into my perspective: with knowledge comes power. Seeing my time laid bare made me kind of angry. Not at any one activity or thing, and certainly at no one but myself. Sure, there were plenty of things staring back at me from those pages that brought me happiness, including time spent shuttling children to activities or exercising with friends. But there were also a lot of activities that seemed to have arbitrarily found their way into my life, demanding time that, if I was being truly honest with myself, I didn't want to give to them. I now had the knowledge. And now I needed to take the power into my own hands.

Exercise: Audit Your Life

Before you can rearrange or add anything to your Legacy List, you must first understand where your time is currently going. Just as an accountant would audit every penny you spend to help you create a better budget, you need to account for every minute of time you spend to be able to find more time for what will build your legacy.

Follow the following steps and then hang on to what you create. We will use it as a base for other exercises in this book—all of which will lead you to creating your Legacy List and a plan for its execution.

Time to Write It Down
Steps for Auditing Your Life

1. Grab paper and several colors of pens or markers, or be ready to color code your list electronically. You'll need at least five colors.

2. Open a single calendar component in your life. This could be a handwritten planner, Google calendar, a calendar mobile app, or anywhere you document your time. You likely have multiple sources, but just start with one.

3. Pick a typical week in your life (if you are doing this exercise on vacation, for example, do not use that week) and write out everything happening in it, and on what day and at what time. Assign the amount of time a task takes directly next to it, and make sure you include the full time. For example, if you work an eight-hour day but it takes you 30 minutes to drive there and back, assign nine hours to your workday, or list the commute separately. I wrote mine out as a seven-day week with items written on each day. Use a different color depending on the category. Some categories I suggest include:

   Work

Spouse/Children/Pets

Extended Family Obligations

Exercise/Hobbies

Volunteerism

Miscellaneous (doctor appointments, car maintenance, paying bills, haircuts, etc.)

4. Repeat Step 3 for all of your calendar sources.

5. Spend some time thinking of what time commitments are not reflected in your calendar sources. Is your work commute listed? Or picking up kids from school? Or grocery shopping (or ordering them online)? Add in a time estimate for as many of these tasks as possible.

6. Glance through your calendars for several more weeks into the future and add anything else that may not have appeared on the week of your focus. Consider monthly and yearly obligations, and add those in.

7. Total up the number of hours weekly, monthly, and yearly that you spend on each category.

8. Hang on to the list to use in the next chapter.

4

UNCOVERING YOUR TRUE CALLING

Goal-setting is an excellent exercise in ambition and optimism. It's great to set your sights on new and wonderful things on the horizon but the accomplishment of those new goals takes time, effort, and the shifting of priorities. It's not as simple as dropping some things and adding others, though. The literal time in our schedule is not all that should determine our choices for how we spend it. We should also place emphasis on how we align with the "why" of how we want to live our lives.

Goals require grounding. Chasing something shiny can feel inspiring on the surface, but a goal without a root grounded in a solid "why" will always take an uphill battle to accomplish. A surface level goal, like spending more time with our family or going to the gym more often, does give us some information, however, that can help us get to the core of that why.

I had a lot of deconstructing to do when I decided to determine my "why" in life. To get to the bottom of it, I first needed to get honest with myself about how I wanted to spend this one precious life here on earth. This meant taking a hard look at my life audit and determining what on the list needed to remain, what needed to go, and what were totally missing. For what felt like the first time in my entire life, I allowed myself to look more closely at my motivation for the scheduled items on my current calendar, and my goals.

What I discovered is that we assume a lot based on what we think we know about societal norms, and even our understanding of ourselves. For example, a volunteer opportunity that we say "yes" to seems to have easy motivation—we want to help the organization or individual who needs it. But that's a flat approach to it, that only reveals the very top layer of understanding. It doesn't really tell us much about ourselves, and why we personally feel connected to that opportunity to do good.

As I started to look at my own audited list of how I was spending my time, I started to feel uneasy. There were plenty of things on that list that were necessary and essential to my own wellness and that of my children—taking them to school, picking them up from school, working to contribute to my large family's finances, doing laundry, grocery shopping, and a whole slew of other activities that though mundane, added up to a lot of time.

The uneasiness didn't come from fulfilling obligations and responsibilities of the life I'd chosen and was trying to foster. The uneasiness came from *the rest* of what was on my list—the social, fitness, volunteer, and dozens of other things I'd at one time said "yes" to that filled my days. There were flickers of the person I wanted to be buried in there, but it was going to take a really big shovel to unearth them and make them shine. I wondered as I squinted at my pages of audit notes: *Where am I in all of this? When do I feel most fulfilled? What am I missing?*

And even though there was nothing sinister in my colorful chicken scratch notes, looking at my life laid out that way, down to its bare bones, felt wrong. It was almost worse that my responsibilities and calendar were so full of nice things. There was nothing specific that stood out as being a "Oh, I really shouldn't be doing that" type of thing. No glaringly toxic people or situations I should remove myself from, no horrible habits that needed to be weeded out. It was all a bunch of nice things that had stacked on top of each other over the years, cluttering my time and schedule, and burying the initial activities that existed.

Duty Versus Obligation

Something slowly began to dawn on me—duty and obligation are not the same as following an aligned path, no matter how noble the acts or commitments.

It doesn't matter if you are the nicest, most unselfish, giving person on the planet. If you are not acting nicely or selflessly or generously because you are aligned with that "why," you are doing it for the wrong reasons. And eventually, your impact in those spaces will be limited.

Aligned commitments have the potential to change everything in your life. They are where you will feel the most fulfilled and where your impact will organically overflow to benefit the rest of the world. You owe it to yourself to exist and act in alignment. And if you are wholly and relentlessly living with that goal in mind, the rest of the world will automatically benefit. You won't need to manufacture something good to leave behind; it will present itself, or even create itself, from the overflow of your alignment.

This idea of duty versus alignment has hung like a heavy shadow over me for more than a decade.

When our oldest daughter (a 17-year-old at the time of writing this book) was a toddler, my parents from Indiana visited us in Florida. As my dad watched my daughter politely interact with the other kids on the playground, waiting her turn and helping the kids around her who needed extra encouragement, the proud grandpa smiled at me and said, "She really reminds me of you as a kid. You've always had such a sense of duty."

It was meant as a compliment, and he really was proud of her, of both of us, in that statement.

But the phrase stung. "Sense of duty." In those three short words I felt my entire personality summed up—the entire way I had always chosen to live my life. Is that what I was doing with my life? Was I making choices on how I spent my time based on a sense of duty?

On its surface, it didn't sound so bad. I mean, if no one ever had a sense of duty, nothing would ever get accomplished. It's why we use the word when talking about our civic duty to vote or serve on a jury, or the duty our military has to protect our lives and livelihoods. When used to describe those tasks that are larger than life, that weigh more heavily than the average, everyday tasks, duty is a solemn oath. It's something to wear like a badge of honor, because it is one.

But the power of duty is dimmed when we are using it as a way to describe our everyday lives, or the things on our list that we just go through the motions to accomplish. Do we really have a duty to ensure that everyone in the room is feeling good about the meeting we are managing? Do we really have a duty to sign up for the bounce house at the school carnival? Do we really have a duty to take on the problems and trials of others? In some cases, the answer might be yes. But to just blindly do something, anything, without connecting it to our very being and the core of who we want to be—or to passively excuse our actions as ones of duty—is not admirable.

It wasn't the word "duty" that Dad had used that was rubbing me the wrong way. It was the underlying motivation—*my* underlying motivation. It hurt my feelings because something inside of me didn't want to be a person who did *everything* out of a sense of duty. I wanted to be a person making change and positively impacting the world because I was actively choosing the places I spent my time and energy. I didn't want to be tethered to guilt or obligation, or responsibility for others' success or happiness. I wanted to improve lives and the world by showing what that could look like as myself, being myself.

When Dad made that comment, I realized that my motivation for many things in my life was in the wrong place. I hadn't been actively trying to make the world a better place because of a deep internal calling. I had been going through the motions of that mask in order to accommodate others and do what I thought I "should" do.

Should Do or Called to Do

There's a big difference between what we think we should do and what we know we are called to do. And what we are called to do takes work to uncover. Sure, there are clues that crop up from the time we are born as to who we are, and what aligns with our natural gifts. And if we were able to immediately follow those clues without abandon, maybe we could get to our true calling quickly and live a life that aligned closely with it.

But we are human, living in a civilized society, where our routines, norms, and paths are already preset to a degree. Can we be anything we want to be? I believe we can—otherwise I wouldn't be writing this book. And every person has preset advantages or disadvantages based on things outside of their control as a child—what country they live in, who their parents are, the amount of material advantages they can access.

This is not an excuse for anyone. I personally know people who have had the odds stacked against them since their literal birth who have found the pathways to improving their situations (not without plenty of difficulties along the way). I also know people who have had access to worldly advantages from a safe home life to wealth, who have squandered it. The point is, no matter who we are, our initial light is eventually dimmed by the outside world.

I have five children who live in my house, and I've seen it happen to them—despite all my awesome parenting tricks to try to keep them being their true, weird, and wonderful selves. Look, middle school happens. So do the teenage years. And there are a whole lot of other reasons people feel self-conscious being fully themselves.

But aside from individual factors that influence us, I have bigger questions. Do humans as a whole species inherently have the wherewithal to follow our internally aligned path? Does our brain want us to discover ourselves, and keep rediscovering ourselves, over and over in life? Or has it evolved to protect us from standing out too much? Is finding true alignment at odds with who we are as evolutionary beings? And if so, this is something we have to acknowledge to combat it and allow our higher-level thinking to overpower what biologically is happening in our minds.

And it isn't just our chemical makeup that can add fuel to the fire burning away our inner being. It's the mixed messaging we receive from the world around us. Phrases like "Just do you" and "You are enough" are lovely sentiments. But in our hustle culture, they are often a far cry from what we actually do in our day-to-day lives. And do any of us really know what just doing "us" looks like? Or *how* we are enough? It seems like those answers would be inherent, but when I stopped to examine my life and what "just doing me" really looked like, I couldn't immediately conjure a clear image.

If we could find and grasp our true alignment at the start of our lives, maybe our own trajectory and the world as a whole would look a whole lot different. The real us would never leave and we could simply find ways to bolster that person from Day One. So we let survival instincts take over, rightfully so, and by the time we've somewhat learned the ins and outs of being human, our true self has already been influenced by the world around us.

Trying to find the root of who we really are underneath it all is difficult after you've lived life for awhile. Your slate is no longer blank. You are a compilation of everything the world has taught, or untaught, you. To get back to the heart of it all, you have to get back to that original slate, which is now covered up with layers of experiences, outside opinions, societal expectations, and even trauma. The longer you live, the more challenging it becomes to see the slate at all. The core of who you are becomes indistinguishable, buried under proverbial piles of plastic wrappers, charging cables, and junk mail. (You'll have to forgive me, I'm writing in my office and taking examples from the real world around me).

When my dad genuinely complimented me and my parenting on that playground, I was still years away from trying to peel off the layers of life that had enveloped my slate. But the seed was planted. I felt "not right" about that description of me because I knew somewhere deep under all the levels of assimilation and masking, it wasn't really "me."

That Heavy-Blanket Moment

The moment stuck with me for years, clinging to me like a heavy blanket I couldn't get out from underneath. It wasn't until eight years later, when I was processing my mom's Alzheimer's diagnosis and trying to figure out what to do with my own life and direction, that the conversation came flooding back to my brain. It gripped me with panic that, at the time, I couldn't quite explain.

"Do you think I only do things out of a sense of duty?" I asked my unsuspecting husband one day in our home office. I had been spouting off existential questions about life a lot since my mom's diagnosis and he was taking it in stride.

He looked up from his typing and answered, hesitantly, "Yes?"

And the years of pent-up feelings about that single comment on a playground just flooded out of me. I carried on about how I'd always thought of myself as a caring person, and that part of my purpose was to advocate for others, but now I wondered how much of what I did in life was motivated by obligation—by a sense of duty—and how much was motivated by what I really wanted to do.

He listened and then carefully offered, "Well, if no one ever felt a sense of duty, then nothing would ever improve."

And that made a lot of sense to me too. It's why I repeated that logic at the beginning of this whole section.

So I sat with the phrase, and my husband's input, and all the big feelings I had just "word vomited" into my home office. And I thought about what was truly at the root of what was bothering me about that now-years-old observation from someone who loved me a whole lot and had literally known me since the day I was born.

It took a little more soul-searching to put my finger on it, but I finally came face-to-face with it—a sense of duty is not enough. Only doing things out of obligation puts the "whys" of everyone else on your shoulders. To really feel connected to your own purpose and direction, you have to find some of "you" in what you do for others.

It occurred to me, for the very first time ever, that perhaps the best way to benefit others was to identify *my* legacy and chase it. The overflow of that chase, of that success, would directly and indirectly benefit everyone else, too. It wasn't selfish to take a step back from doing things purely for others; it was part of what I was called to do as an individual. I was fulfilling a sacred obligation to myself, and to the rest of my community and the world that I would touch by living authentically.

With sudden clarity I realized that by allowing the "whys" of others to dictate my moves, I was neglecting my own calling. I was selling myself short, and the rest of the world, by not pinning down that purpose and relentlessly pursuing it. This is certainly not the first book to suggest that goals should be grounded in purpose. It's become almost cliche in a journal and affirmations kind of way (I love both of those things, by the way).

The premise is simple—figure out who you want to be, and then pour yourself into being that person. Right, simple, like I said. I've got a stack of guided and free-hand journals on my nightstand, however, that tell a more complicated story. It takes a lot of reflection, questioning, and pushing ourselves to truly begin peeling away the layers of the "who" at the bottom of the proverbial debris pile.

There are certainly things we know about ourselves intuitively, good and bad. For example, I know that I'm a good connector. I can almost instinctively meet a person and know who else in my circle they should also meet to further both of their paths. Even if I didn't *want* to be this person, even if I decided this was a pitfall of my personality, I could not shut off the voices in my head that automatically connect people and opportunities. They would still live in there, whether I said them out loud or not.

Part of my personal Legacy List process, however, has been to create some boundaries around how much time and energy I put into these connections for others. I've had to tell myself, plenty of times, "The connection is enough. Now let it evolve on its own." Or in other instances I've even told myself, *This is not your place to get involved at all. If these people or opportunities are destined for each other, they will find their way without my help.* Which is a hard thing to admit when you are good at connecting *and* like inserting yourself into every situation just to be part of it. It took a lot of soul searching, and owning a Golden Doodle, to recognize this part of my connecting gift that is truly selfish. *You do not need to be part of literally everything* (repeats to Golden Doodle over and over again every day).

I might have a gift for connection but so do other people. And inherently, people have an instinct about what step to take next or who to connect with to further their cause. They don't need me. But by being more selective in *how* I'm connecting, or using my time to do so, the authentic ones that I make are even more meaningful.

Another good/bad part of my personality that I've had to contend with has to do with efficiency, or in some cases, taking shortcuts. On the surface, being efficient or looking for faster paths to completion is not so bad, right? Our brains are literally wired for shortcuts—it's actually how we've survived until this point and how we've made so much human progress. But, as with basically everything I'm discussing in this book, it's my *motivation* for shortcuts that is the source of the problem.

I get so hung up on the end result—on the win, on the box to check, on the accolades, on the destination—that I neglect important steps on the path. And when I do that—when I'm always looking for the fastest way to an end goal—I miss out on a whole lot as I go along. It also leads to less quality in my end products and more mistakes made along the way. I know, I know. Mistakes are part of the learning process, but when they are made because of haste and not because of genuinely taking a vested chance, they are mistakes that could have been avoided.

So part of my Legacy List journey has been to stop being so end-goal driven, and start looking for more ways to enjoy my actual process. Even with this book. It's easy to get caught up in publisher deadlines (which, thank goodness for them, or I'd never get anything finished) or the word count I should strive for each day instead of taking the time to delve into the true reason I'm writing this at all. The "why" behind this book, which is to inspire others to find their true calling and align with it.

This book's "why" is not dependent on deadlines or word counts. It is an entity all its own that requires no shortcuts. Structure and focus? Absolutely. Assembly-style writing that adheres to a construct, instead of a gut feeling? Absolutely not.

I mention both of these personality gifts/curses here because in identifying my "why" for my Legacy List, I realized them both. And when I'm using the gifts of connection and efficiency as a means to meet external expectations, they get in the way of the internal work I am doing. It's not the personality trait or even the action that is at issue. It's the motivation. It's the whole "sense of duty" of it all. Combining my personality propensities with a grounded, aligned reason is a powerful punch that will make resounding waves in my life and those around me.

And it will for you, too. But to find the reason we tick, the purpose behind all that we do, we have to identify our motivation and then decide if it's aligned, or part of the mask we wear.

That's what this next exercise is all about—examining our motivations to discover our true "why" and use that to propel our Legacy List.

Exercise: Find Your Why

If finding your why feels like a heavy task—that's good. That means you are approaching the answer to this question with the weight it deserves. I'd love to say that there is no wrong answer but that's not exactly the truth. Perhaps a better way to phrase it is that there could be multiple right answers. None of us can see the future and none of us is always aligned at our very core every second of every day.

Don't feel overwhelmed at needing to find the right answer; just be vigilant in weeding out any motivation, obligation, or "sense of duty" that leads you to wrong answers.

By the end of this exercise, you should be able to name the core reasons you do what you do. Then we'll look at how your current schedule and commitments are either feeding into your "why" or deterring from it.

Time to Write It Down

Let's get started asking the right questions to get to the core of who you are and why you move through your life.

1. Take out a clean sheet of paper, or open a new document on any screen.

2. Type or write the phrase: I (action here) because.... This should be anything you do in your regular schedule that you've identified in your audit. You can also fill in the same blank several times with different reasons. Examples could look like:

   I work at XYZ company because I need to earn an income to afford life.

   I work at XYZ company because they offer a flexible schedule and I can still pick my kids up from school.

   I work out three mornings per week because it keeps me strong.

   I volunteer at my kids' school because I want to be part of their school environment.

   I volunteer at my kids' school because I feel pressured to do it.

Each thing you do may have multiple reasons. Be sure to consult your life audit and schedule so that you don't leave anything out. Even things that seem small matter, such as making a meal for yourself or your family every day or a few times per week. And remember, many of your answers may not feel meaningful or may even seem shallow. Do not write down what you *think* you should say is your motivation. Write down the *truth,* just for you. This will help you determine what aligns with the person you really want to be, and the legacy you want to leave, and what does not belong in the future version of your life. Take as much time with this part of the exercise as you need.

3. Once you feel like you have a pretty exhaustive list of your tasks and motivations, read back over them. Using a pen, marker, or highlighter (or a highlighter feature on your device), circle or highlight the motivations that feel most real to you—the ones that most align with the person you *want* to be.

4. Now take a different-colored writing device or highlight feature and circle or highlight all of the motivations that feel completely off from

the direction you want your life to take. This could include any motivation that is prompted by an outside force, such as pressure from your friends or community.

5. Look over these circles or highlights and see what's left on your list. Are there any that did not fit into either definition? Are there any that are somewhere in the middle? Leave those as is, but read over them. It's possible that these are undecided motivations in your mind—and at the very least, you should notice them.

6. Loop back to the motivations that seemed "off." What about those seem unaligned? Is there anything listed there that you would remove completely if you could? At the bottom of your document, write out a few thoughts as to why these motivations do not fit.

7. Now look at the aspirations you noted as admirable motivations, that feel like the core of who you are trying to be as a human. Is there a common thread? Do they focus on your natural gifts? Are they family or friendship based? What about them feels right to you? Write down similarities and overall thoughts as to why you circled or highlighted these areas.

8. Now that you have looked over what your current tasks and motivations look like, it's time to dream a little bit. What motivation do you wish you saw more on your list? Maybe it's something tangible, like wanting to live a healthier lifestyle to improve your quality of life and that of the people in your circle. Maybe it's something a little more abstract, like wanting to leave the world a better place than how you found it. Think about who you truly want to be in this one precious life—and write down a few important core values that you want to continue building, or start from scratch.

9. Once you've allowed yourself to search this part of you, write a few sentences that are your "why." This is similar to a statement of purpose or a motto. Start with the words: "My 'why' in life is" and then write out the truest of the motivations that you've discovered in this exercise. Why do you do what you do? What do you *want* to be your purpose here, and what will you leave behind?

10. Circle, highlight, or otherwise accent the most important words in that "why" statement so they stand out to you.

Keep this "why" statement close. We'll need it for the rest of the book—and for the steps you take after reading it.

5

LETTING GO TO CREATE YOUR LEGACY

Personal growth often includes adding things to our proverbial plate. When we visualize growth, we often see images of flowers rising from seedy soil, or rainbows stretching across the sky. At its core, growth means to get bigger, add more, *be* more. But what if I told you that true growth is less about addition, and more about subtraction? It's a hard concept to reconcile, particularly in a world that keeps upping the base requirements for what it means to live a purposeful life. Each generation of humans adds a layer of life necessities, making it harder to keep up with all of those demands.

Which is why I found myself at an impasse on my Legacy List journey. I could see all the places where important things were missing from my life. I just needed to *add* them to my life. But when? And how?

And with what resources? I didn't feel inspired by my list. I felt overwhelmed.

I knew what I needed to do to make the whole thing less daunting—get rid of things on the list.

I needed to let go of my death grip of everything I had said "yes" to and free up more space for my Legacy List. I really didn't want to do that though. It's hard to end obligations, especially if it means disappointing people. I didn't want to be the cause of anyone's job or task to be harder as a result of me not doing what I'd always done. But even this thought was a selfish one because it was based more on my fear of disappointing people than on me caring how they would manage without me.

I tried waking up at 4 a.m. or spending less time on Facebook or in my texts to accommodate tasks associated with my new lease on life. That worked, sort of, but quickly reminded me that time isn't the only resource we need to introduce new elements into our life. We also need energy, both physically and mentally.

It became clear that all of the self-discovery I'd made, and all of my progress to uncover what my Legacy List should look like, would be wasted without culling and editing my life. I had to make space for the time and energy of the emphasis I wanted.

And it's been a bit of a slow process. The concept of letting go of something before I can embrace something new has taken a lot of work for me to embrace and execute. And sometimes I still say "yes" too quickly in the moment to new commitments. But one major lesson I've learned in my Legacy List journey is that you have to make space for what matters most on your docket. You cannot create more seconds in a minute or more minutes in the hours of your day. Sure, you could sleep less (been there) or give up your free time (if there's any to give) to accommodate new priorities, but often there is life clutter that can be reorganized and cleaned up to make the space we need.

The hardest part of creating, strengthening, and growing my Legacy List has been culling my schedule. And not because there are a lot of things that I was sad to remove, but because I got really angry when I started to see the way my time had been parsed out to things I didn't want to lend it to. Culling my list reminded me of a good rage-cleaning session where I started out refolding towels in my linen closet and soon found myself scrubbing the baseboards in the hallway, dusting a ceiling fan's blades, and emptying the junk drawer in the adjoining bathroom—all while seething that any of those chores had come to that point. As I noticed one thing that needed adjusting on my list, I quickly noticed several more. I started to ask myself, *Why am I doing this? Am I the right person for this? Why am I spending so much time on this particular task when I have zero time for my heart projects?*

A Pattern of Layering

I started to notice a pattern of layering. My jam-packed schedule had not been hand-delivered to me at age 18 for me to maintain throughout adulthood. It had become unwieldy, like vines encroaching, over time and through several decisions I had made, all with the best of intentions. Nothing on my schedule was illegal, or even unvirtuous. But I felt panicked looking at it, in all its tiered glory, for I knew that the undoing of the knotted obligations would take some time, tough conversations, and potentially even mean some grieving.

I also had a enlightenment moment in this rage cleaning of my schedule. I looked at some of the responsibilities listed—some that had been on my list for years—and realized that nothing we say "yes" to has to be forever. A job, a volunteer opportunity, even relationships—a "yes" once does not mean we have to maintain it for all of time. And we can be happy with what we've accomplished while still setting a boundary for ourselves and moving forward.

There were bullet points in my schedule that were ready to pass on to someone else. And not just ready to, I realized that in many cases, a fresh person could do a better job than me. This applied to some of my hobbies, volunteer obligations, and even regular work. Though I had once chosen each and every item on my list, I did not need to keep choosing them indefinitely. And this brought me a surge of relief, knowing that I had some tough choices to make but that they were just that—choices I could make.

I realize there are some obligations we cannot walk away from. I hope it goes without saying that children in our care are not commitments we can simply cross off our list. And that ending adult relationships, whether romantic, friendships, or even toxic family scenarios, deserve pause and require professional help to navigate. Certain things are sacred on every list. But the key is to understand that not everything falls into that sacred category. You don't have to keep your word forever on something you agreed to do or added to your schedule once upon a time. If it no longer serves you, it is probably no longer serving the people, places, or things you originally wanted to help. It's okay to admit that. Not everything needs you the way you think it does. And ouch, does that hurt to truly consider. But it's true.

I also realized that the items on my list that felt too heavy were already seeing lack of engagement from me. They were already suffering—whether that was in lack of fresh creativity from me, delayed timelines, or just simply less getting done. In some cases, I was hanging on by a thread, wanting to fulfill my obligations with minimal participation. I was too afraid to let go of it, but apparently perfectly fine half-assing it and taking everyone else along for that ride.

What if the commitments I was no longer aligned with would be better off without me? I was humbled by that thought. These tasks and obligations didn't *need* me to thrive—and I was probably standing in the way of that by remaining "committed" to the cause, tasks, or duties. When you spot these things on your list, don't second-guess them. Those are deal-breakers for your own Legacy List, and the lists of others. And that is actually *okay* and everyone is going to be just fine. It is okay to turn a one-time "yes" into an eventual "no." Keep that in mind when we get to the exercise at the end of this chapter.

What We Do for Money

I want to pause and talk about money for a few minutes. I know, I know. How very crass of me. We're talking about dreams here—so why bring up something as realistic and stressful as money? Look, money really does make the world go 'round, and it does dictate a lot of what we choose in our day-to-day life. It's easy for me to tell you that if your job doesn't align with your calling, you should cross it off your list—but it will be harder to chase your dream if you are hungry or without a home. There is a difference between the work we do out of necessity and the commitments we add for fluff. I do not recommend quitting your job right away. But building a path that allows you to take that step down the road is better than not identifying those markers in advance.

Sometimes tuning into the song of your legacy, however, will force your hand. I've been fired three times in my life: once was my first real job out of college when I was 23, once was when I tried during Covid days to balance two full-time jobs at the same time at age 38, and another was more recently, within a month from writing this section of the book. I was 42.

All of these instances have a few things in common. The first is that I was legitimately *fired* from all three. Not laid off. Not asked to leave because of restructuring or downsizing. But actually asked to leave, and immediately, because I was no longer a fit for the job, and that fact had become clear to everyone (including me). Depending who you ask, these firings were performance-based, though I'd argue it was more of a shift of my attitude toward performing my tasks that was the problem. And in each instance, I was in a transitory period of my life—with more on my mind than usual to distract me from work.

My first firing from a "real job" after college was really what you'd expect. Armed with my degree in

English Studies, I set out to find my fortune in the lucrative field of journalism. I had no experience as a reporter—hadn't even written for my high school or college newspaper—so I realized early on that it would be a tough position to crack. But I liked to tell stories, true stories, and hear about the lives of others.

It was 2005 and newspapers were still in their Golden Era, not yet engulfed by the voracity of digital news. People still read a physical newspaper, including people in their 20s, like me. Later in my career, I'd discover that just about any newspaper brand would hire me to cover a story if I was willing to drive to an obscure city council meeting or interview a local small business owner based on little but my ability to drive to those places. But in 2005, these venues were still particular. Picky, even. For example, they preferred their journalists to have a degree in journalism or at least some experience in the field. I mean. Scoff.

So I started to think of other ways I could use my college degree—the promise of financial success in America for millennials—and still stay in the general vicinity of the English Studies printed on my official Ball State University bachelor's degree. I was browsing the classified want ads for employment in a copy of the Indianapolis Star when a job jumped right off the page at me: Editor at a prominent pharmaceutical magazine. Well, it sounded prominent. I had truthfully never heard of it, but another area I had zero experience in was pharmaceuticals.

I don't remember much else except that the annual pay was $26,000, which really was nothing for a 23-year-old English major to turn their nose up to in 2005.

I landed an interview for the following week and tried my best to research all of the buzz words listed in the job description, many of which were rather specific to the pharmaceutical industry. I had access to the internet since around 1995, and that decade showed me that anything I needed to research was really just a few keystrokes away. So I found digital versions of the journal online to study and did a deep dive (as much as I could in 2005) on the company origins and who I would most likely be talking with at my interview. I wanted to be ready. This $26,000 per year job was *all* mine!

When I arrived at the office for my interview, I noticed the crop of young people, like me, who filled the office. My bosses were significantly older than everyone else, probably even in their (gasp) 40s. It was much later when I realized what a red flag that actually was. But at that moment, it made me feel at ease. The word "American" was in the title of the journal, but I soon learned this version was a knockoff of the British original. It all seemed a little "off" but my work experience to that date had consisted of waitressing, babysitting, and selling passes to people who wanted to park at the beach in my hometown. There was a lot I didn't know about office culture. Or publishing. Or pharmaceuticals.

I was hired within the week of my interview and really couldn't believe my good fortune. I was going to have the word "editor" in my job title. I even got to write a little editor's note at the start of the bi-monthly print version of the product with my headshot. In the September/October edition, I wrote about the leaves changing. In the November/December edition, I wrote about holiday traditions. I'm sure you can piece together how the months following those looked and read. This was a serious job and I was a serious worker.

It didn't take too long to discover that my excitement over the actual editing of the product was null and void. I was more of a content scheduler—with much of my days spent cold calling scientists and asking them to write for our journal, for free. My job was less about the quality of those articles and more about the money that the advertising team could make off of them. When articles were written, they were sold against for advertising space—which wasn't my job, but I certainly felt that pressure. Often the sales team, some who were even younger and more fresh-faced than me, would give me names of scientists, researchers, or other leaders who they really hoped I could get to agree to write an article because it would sell well. It was then up to me to convince said writer to lend their name, credibility, and time to our journal.

Needless to say, this was an uphill task, often resulting in hearing the word "no" much more often than "yes." I felt like the telemarketers that my dad used to hang up on when they called us during family dinner. No one knew who I was or why they should write for us. The reasons for the denials made sense, of course. No time outside of actual research to write. No monetary compensation for that time. Six-month-long research trips that would take them to an island without an internet connection. You know, things like that. I was of course respectful of the "no" responses—seeing no real upside for these authors, if I was being honest. The little editing I did was relegated to signing off on tear sheets of the journal layout before it went to print, looking for errors in typography or spacing. I actually loved those days because I actually looked at a nearly-complete project and put my own stamp on it, however small.

Eventually though, the "nos" caught up to me when it came to the sales team and my bosses. How could they expect to make money if I wasn't hooking the names they needed? I remember feeling really badly about it, too. I wished I could magically make the consent of the writers appear. A wiser version of myself would be kinder to this past me, realizing that my job title did not match the tasks being asked of me. But as a young person at my first "real job," it was a heavy weight to feel like I was disappointing my colleagues and not doing a good job.

When the Cards Fall

It was a Monday morning when my guilt, their demands, and the overall uphill climb of my tasks finally came to a head. Nearly everyone in the office was gone that week, at a pharmaceutical conference in San Francisco. One of my favorite parts of the job was traveling to conferences in exotic places like Orlando and Washington, DC. I was surprised when I wasn't included in the California conference trip because generally as editor, the sales team had a long list of clients and places they wanted me to hit up while there. I enjoyed staying in nice hotels and meeting people. That part of the job was probably my favorite: having a reason to introduce myself to new people and chat with them. Conferences provided that on overload.

But it was also expensive to send an entire office team to San Francisco from Indianapolis, and after all, *someone* needed to stay and work. The administrative assistant who worked at the front desk had stayed behind, and so had the designer who really had no need to be at a conference. My bosses stayed behind too. Usually they didn't go to conferences, leaving the fatigue of travel and $20 per day food allowances to us young employees. It didn't strike me as odd at all that I was in the group that stayed behind. *Other people had been the ones to stay behind for past conferences, right?*

But as I was getting my clothes ready that Sunday night for an early Monday morning drive into the Circle City, I wished I didn't have to go. It was early May, my birthday week, and it was supposed to be one of the first truly warm and sunny days of the year. I considered calling in sick, something I hadn't done at all in the six months I had worked there. This was mostly because there was no official sick policy and it was unclear if I would be paid to stay home. But when my alarm went off, I shook off my slumber and went through the early morning pre-work motions of a person who is really dreading going to their job. This included sitting in my comfy pajamas and drinking my homemade coffee as long as possible before squeezing into the itchy polyester dress clothes I'd purchased at an outlet store.

My apartment had a small balcony that overlooked a pond with a spouting fountain right in the middle. I sat there a few minutes extra that morning, listening to the consistent whoosh of the water hitting the pool below it and the baby birds that seemed to be invisibly multiplying all around me. I really didn't want to go to work. But as mentioned, I had to go to work that day.

I arrived at work after a 45-minute drive battling Monday morning traffic on I-465 to find my bosses already there and in their giant shared office space. It was odd for them to arrive early—it was only 8:45 a.m. I nodded at them and greeted the admin who usually showed up a little early, like me, to get in the right headspace before the day got hectic. The designer wasn't there yet.

I had barely set down my car keys on my desk when one of the boss pair asked me to come into the office where they sat. He just tapped on the glass with his knuckles and motioned for me to join them. I groaned internally. It was too early and I was not nearly caffeinated enough to handle a meeting with them. I grabbed a small steno notepad off my desk and a pen and walked briefly into the hallway to get to their entrance point.

As soon as I sat down and looked at both of their faces, I knew what was happening. Suddenly the obvious nature of staying behind from the conference, and my bosses being in early on a Monday, and all of the beautiful details of the outdoors that I'd noticed just an hour prior landed on me with a proverbial thud. I nearly stood up and raised my hands in surrender, as if to say "Say no more. I'll just be getting my things and going." But my body and face were frozen in the uncomfortable, cheap office chair, one hand tightly gripping my pen and the other, my notebook.

I heard the words swirling, something about performance expectations not being met, about how the role was no longer a fit for me, about how I could clearly do better at a different job. Certain words cut through my paralysis: "nothing personal" and "other roads for you" were a few. And then suddenly, it was silent. They were looking at me, awaiting a response.

And the only thing I could think to say was, "Can I go now?"

No arguments. No defending myself. No pointing out the many flaws I saw in their workplace. I wasn't scared to say any of those things. I mean, I truly had nothing to lose. It was just that I didn't care. I had already checked out of the job and now all I could think about was getting home to brew a second pot of coffee and sit on my balcony, enjoying the omnipresent sounds of the invisible baby birds.

One of the bosses simply answered, "Yes" and gestured toward the office door. I stumbled back to my desk, passing the designer who had just arrived.

"I Got Fired"

"I got fired," I told her, matter-of-factly and loudly. Her jaw dropped but I didn't stick around to see if she could scrape it off the floor. At my desk I was so busy packing up what little I'd accumulated in the short time I worked there that I didn't even notice one of the evil boss twins standing at the corner of my desk. No, not standing. Hovering. I paused and looked him in the eye.

"Yes?" I questioned.

He said nothing. But looked away from my stare to his feet.

"Oh, I see. You're going to watch me pack up everything and make sure I don't steal anything, right? Or that I don't destroy company property, like this stapler here or those expensive cameras over there?" I said, my voice even and monotone.

"Actually," he said, "I just came to get your office key."

I grabbed my purse from the desk drawer and dramatically slammed it onto the desk. I pulled the snap at the top apart and thus began an emptying of my purse, that I'm sure he would've rather not seen. Chapstick, straw wrappers, sticks of gum, sanitary napkins, an extra pair of socks, movie tickets and crumbs from movie-theatre popcorn, a few Swedish fish candies, and more—all laid out and leaving residue on the desk as I dug for the office key. I had used it maybe twice since working there and hadn't seen it in literal months. I started to panic, wondering if it wasn't in my purse after all. Not because I cared all that much but because I simply did not want to drive back over there, ever, to return it later.

Finally, pressed firmly into the seam of the bottom of my purse was that golden key. My ticket *out* of that place. I grabbed it triumphantly and blew off my personal blend of purse dust. I set it on the corner of the desk nearest my now ex-boss and started tossing everything back in my purse, even the straw wrappers. Those were *my* straw wrappers and I was damned if anything of mine was going to be left behind. Things were starting to get silly. I could feel my cool nature spiraling. I had to get out of there.

I haphazardly threw what was left in a cardboard box that had been sitting on the floor, tucked back behind my desk, conveniently. The one-half of my former bosses lingered as I did so, a few steps back.

I hoisted the box onto the front of my body and walked toward the office door. When I strolled by the administrative assistant, she looked up and me with wide eyes and started to open her mouth but saw the same half-boss trailing behind me, and snapped her jaw shut, diverting her eyes.

"I was fired," I told her anyway. "I already turned in my key."

And with that, I walked out of that office and away from my first "professional" job without merit, or honor. My black shirt was covered in purse pixie dust and my awkward box shifted each time I took a step forward, the personal knickknacks inside clattering against each other. I was a mess, really. But man, was I happy to be walking away from that once-golden-hued opportunity.

It's weird, as I'm writing this now, to think of the way we sometimes suddenly walk away from things in our lives. Workplaces that are ingrained in our routine, or the homes that once sheltered us. The places that make up our whole existences, just left behind, never to return to again.

I've never set foot in that building since the day I was fired. And have never missed it. But at one time it housed me for 40-plus hours per week, and made possible my first apartment's rent and the gas I needed to buy to get there and back five days per week. For 261 days out of the year, it was my morning destination and at the end of the workday, the place from where I'd go home. And then one random Monday morning I went there unknowingly one final time.

And all of those hours, those days, those destinations are somehow swallowed up by the next thing. And though there are definitely places that I'm nostalgic for sometimes, I'm comforted by the gift of retrospect. Any opportunity that leaves is replaceable.

But I digress—back to that day. As I drove back toward my apartment, putting distance between me and my former employer, I felt lighter. The guilt and unhappiness I'd been carrying around like a weight floated off. I didn't know what I would do next, but I knew I was driving toward something better. It was the first time in my life that being reprimanded (in the biggest way possible) felt good. I wasn't embarrassed and I wasn't feeling negative about it. I was actually happy about it. And that's because something inside knew that the universe took care of something I should have done myself.

It took getting fired from that job for me to find my way to journalism. I started working at a small-town Indiana newspaper the very next week as a county government and education beat reporter. That job took me to Orlando, where I answered phones and worked in research at a "Top 20" newspaper, which took me to a "Top 5" newspaper in Chicago, which eventually brought me back to Florida where I launched a successful freelance journalism and writing business from home, typing away between school pickups and blogging about parenthood and entrepreneurship.

And now that story is part of this book. I tell it not to glorify slacking off at your job but rather to drive home this point: what is *not* meant for you will make itself clear and it won't feel as badly as you thought it would when the cards fall.

The Third Time

But another point, and one that I am still trying to master, is that waiting for your life to implode when you know something is off is not advisable either. The story I just told could have been basically told in a similar fashion regarding an incident that happened just months before I am writing this, when I was fired for the third time in my life (I know I skipped the second one, but you can just infer).

Instead of showing up for work on a Monday morning, I had a scheduled Zoom meeting on a Monday afternoon. And instead of returning the key at the bottom of my purse, I printed out a FedEx packing slip to send in my work-issued laptop. I had stayed at a job longer than it served me or my team. I had stayed because it was easier and the pay was much more than the $26,000 annually. I thought I could hold on to a role that I had outgrown long enough for it to be more convenient for me to step away. But the Legacy List I had written, and was actively pursuing, was pulling me further and further away from the job that once seemed like a perfect fit for me and my family.

I had edited my life five years earlier but allowed things to creep back in that had no place in my new alignment. So I revisited my list and edited it again. I looked for ways to remove any of the weeds, especially the good-intentioned ones, that had found their way to my schedule again. I also took a moment to soak in this life lesson, served up to me nearly 20 years after the first one.

Instead of frantically searching for a find/replace job on LinkedIn, I returned to my Legacy List. I looked at the ambitions on it that were already succeeding, and the dreams in my heart that I had not yet had time to address. And when I ran the finances on my "little performing arts studio," I discovered that it was making money—and had the potential to make a lot more, if only I had the time to make that happen. It wasn't time to refill my schedule with new commitments unaligned with the life I was trying to create—it was time to double down on that life and take the universe's lessons seriously.

Letting go of anything familiar is difficult. Even the things we release that bring relief come with a pinch of "what if." What if I'm walking away at the wrong time? What if I never recover from this? What if I'm ruining my own life and the life of literally everyone I know? But editing, and re-editing, your life is necessary for it to flourish, despite the what ifs.

Exercise: Editing Your Life

Adding to our schedules is not actually that hard. We do it gradually—with a "yes" here, or a "I'd be happy to help" there. We pile on our commitments, one thing at a time, and it's actually quite easy to get buried under the mire.

Trying to dig out from that pile-on is the challenge. Remember that audit we did back in Chapter 2? The one where we listed all the obligations and responsibilities in our lives? It's time to take that back out, whether you wrote it on a legal pad with pen, or on journal pages with pastel markers, or typed it onto the screen of your computer or in the notes in your phone.

It's time to look at what is no longer serving you on that list and start crossing things off. Make no mistake, simply crossing something off the list won't actually eliminate it from your schedule or your life. But for the sake of this exercise, and the ones that will follow, plan to cross items off your list. There's a certain process we will follow for it though. so don't get too Sharpie happy just yet.

Things to remember in this exercise:

- It's nothing personal. Try to remove guilt from what you cross off. It does not mean you don't care about the obligations or people connected to them. This exercise is about getting real about what you see as the path for ***your*** legacy.

- No one is going to see this. Unless you share it with someone else of your own volition, no one will even know what you are crossing off. Eliminate as if no one is watching (because no one is).

- Good does not equal correct. There may be a slew of good-intentioned or virtuous items on your list that include volunteer commitments, church obligations, or even extra family tasks (planning that giant family vacation, for example, or always taking the lead on planning family reunions).

There are a lot of things we do out of "duty" that may not align with our path. This exercise is about *you.* Cross off what are out of alignment, even the "good" ones. Later on we will determine which are actually options to eliminate immediately, what may take time, and what may need to stick around for now.

Time to Write It Down

Have that life audit ready? Great, let's get started.

1. Open your life audit list from Chapter 2. Have a separate piece of paper ready, or screen open, as well.

2. Reread the items on that list and be honest with yourself. What of those do you wish were *not* there? This is your list so don't feel badly or weigh the feelings of anyone else, at least not for this step.

3. Write these words on the top of the new page: Things I Need to Eliminate.

4. Begin crossing off or eliminating items on your original list by asking yourself, *What would make me feel happy or relieved to eliminate?*

5. Write those items on the other page to save for later.

6

COMMITTING TO A LIFE THAT WILL OUTLIVE YOU

We're taught from an early age to "dream big" and that our current circumstances do not reflect our vast potential. While I am fully a "don't hold me back" personality, I've learned that the best way to get to those big audacious dreams is to start small. It's always most effective to look at what is around us already—and where we can get that foothold—and then dig in. Nothing worthwhile happens overnight, even if it seems like it to you when you look at the lives of others. That job promotion your random acquaintance on social media landed? They got to that point by working at entry-level pay, taking the job seriously, and working hard.

The real estate agent who posts about having a $5 million month? That agent started the work day at 4 a.m. for three years straight, writing contracts and responding to numerous buyer and seller questions.

That performer in your life who seems to *always* get the part? That person thought about quitting many times after being rejected or told "no," but instead joined a class to improve audition techniques and signed up to take private lessons. In those examples, and others, hypothetical acquaintances just keep showing up.

The point is this: for every duck we see floating on the pond, there are a million cute little webbed kicks happening just under the surface. Your Legacy List is going to take work to manifest. It's going to take grit, focus, and a million cute little duck kicks. But you have it in you, or you wouldn't have made it even this far in the book. And you've already put in the work to prepare you to write your Legacy List.

Jumping Off Point

If you like to count or perform division problems, you've likely deciphered that this chapter—this *writing* your Legacy List—is only about halfway into this book. And that's because it is not the culminating act. It is the jumping off point. Once you have this list in place, you will have to apply actionable steps to put it in motion and keep it moving forward throughout your life. The chapters beyond this are designed to help you with the follow-through—to sustain you when the honeymoon phase of this book ends.

I think we've all had moments of extreme inspiration that changed us for the better. It happens to me when I see a musical or play done especially well. I come home almost jittery with endorphins, vowing to have that kind of impact the next time I am cast in a role. It's happened to me when I've attended a live concert or a conference for work or for a hobby. What I see in front of me inspires me on a purely emotional level.

Eventually, most of those feelings fade. Sure I might journal about them—because, let's face it, I'm going to journal about them—but usually the moment of motivation comes and goes. And there's nothing inherently wrong with benefitting from surges of admiration and inspiration. It's okay to just feel those warm, motivating feelings as they engulf you right then. You don't need to act on everything. But there's a reason why things speak to you the way that they do and it's important to pause and recognize them. That's what writing your Legacy List is really all about—working through this current moment of inspiration to make it last.

I hope that something you've written so far or something I've said in these pages has inspired you to chase down some dreams that have been on your heart for some time. Again, the point of writing your Legacy List and living it is multifaceted. No matter how slight the realignment is in your life, know that it matters. Let's get started writing your Legacy List.

Exercise: Write Your Legacy List

Now that we've taken the time to audit our lives, examined that list, identified our passions and path, crossed off the items we really think are in our way to that path, and reflected on it all—the time has come to create our actual Legacy List. Once we've done that, we'll take some time to come up with a strategy and timeline—and some safeguards to keep us on track when the journey is difficult or tumultuous.

We did *all* that in this chapter, so in this task, let yourself get carried away with your own hopes, dreams, and potential. We will iron out the tangible details later.

For this exercise, you need access to everything you have already written, whether in a notebook or on an electronic screen. You need to reference what you've already said, and maybe even make some slight edits, as your Legacy List forms.

Got them all? Okay then. Let's get started writing your Legacy List, step by step. You do not have to complete these tasks in one sitting; if it takes you several sittings, that's okay. Try to finish this within one week of starting it, however. Procrastination and life's distractions are the biggest hindrances to us realizing and following our paths. The world needs your Legacy List in action, now. Today. So prioritize finishing this list, even if you need some breaks in the process.

Time to Write It Down

Step 1. Write a short article about yourself, written 50 years after your death. Assume that you live to be 100, and the letter is dated for 50 years after whatever year you would turn 100.

- Give it a headline and include quotes from living (pretend) people who have been impacted by the legacy you created and left behind.
- Aim for three or four short paragraphs that sum up how the work you did in this life and the ripple effect you created have impacted the world for the better. This impact can be large in scale (curing a disease), more niche (furthering a conversation about the human experience), or very specific to your inner circle (leaving a legacy of encouragement and love for your children and grandchildren).

- Explain in this article exactly what you view your legacy to be, and write about how it looks a half-century after you have left it behind.

Step 2. Look over the words of each exercise so far—from determining "who" you are, or eliminating things from your schedule. Spend as much time as you like reviewing what you already learned about yourself in this Legacy List process. Keep those reflections at the front of your mind as you move into the next step of the exercise.

Step 3. Write your Legacy List. Funnel all that you've just reread about your hopes, dreams, and obligations into the blanks you need to fill in below.

Your Legacy List format should look like this:

> I, (name), know that my life is meaningful and that even after my death, the work I do in this life will matter. This is why I have created my own Legacy List.
>
> I know that I am supposed to (list the number one thing you feel called to do).
>
> I am uniquely qualified for this calling because (list your talents and experiences to say why; don't hold back).

> I will pour more into my path by (list tangible ways you plan to do it).
>
> I will eliminate (list these things).
>
> The work I do will benefit (list as many people, things, or causes that will see a boost because of the work you do).
>
> Leaving a positive legacy is important to me because (remind yourself of all the reasons).
>
> I commit to creating a life that will outlive me, today (date), and will keep returning to this promise as I live this path.

Step 4. Write a letter to yourself, dated the day you write it. Make a promise to yourself in this letter to follow through on your Legacy List, even when it seems difficult. Commit to returning to your Legacy List, again and again, as many times as you need, to make the biggest impact on your world. Talk about your challenges—what might stand in your way? What mentally could impact you? What do you know about yourself that could push you off your path?

For me, pleasing people was a huge obstacle at first. It was *hard* to say no to things that didn't align with the Legacy List I'd set forth. Especially if it seemed like there was room in my schedule. I knew this about myself though, and I *really* felt it the first couple times I declined something that would have normally been a "yes." It was difficult, almost impossible, to say no and realize I disappointed someone. But this was part of my personality I knew I needed to contend with to move to the next level of making my long-term difference in the world.

So I wrote about it in my letter. I called myself out for it. I didn't write a flowery note that boosted my self esteem (though reminding yourself of how great you are *is* something I'd recommend in this step). I spoke frankly with myself about internal and external challenges. And then gently reminded myself of the whole point of doing all of my Legacy List work: to align my actions and energy with the things I've determined I want to leave behind.

I reread this letter often, and have written follow-ups to it as I've walked my Legacy List path and learned more about its reality.

Write this honest letter to your current-day self and keep it near your Legacy List.

7

YOU HAVE TO START SOMEWHERE

Boy do I love a good journaling session. Just me, my coffee, my hopes, my dreams, and my colorful pens. It's a special bubble where no answer is wrong and the sky is the limit. I can write about my challenges, my triumphs, and the things I hope to conquer in the future—all within the safety of my brightly-coded musings.

When I first started my Legacy List journey, my journaling was intense. Not cute, or even reflective—***intense.*** I had a whole list of daily prompts that I'd written myself to answer, as well as free journaling space. I had a copy of a few versions of gratitude journals in my stack that I visited every day. I added a weekly journal to the mix. My best friend and I wrote our own five-year journal and self-published it on Amazon. I had a journal for every span of time imaginable, and free-journaling exercises for those nook-and-cranny moments. I was feeling all the things and making sure I shared the feelings in my writings.

One morning as my husband and I readied our kids for school—packing their lunches and trying to find socks that matched—I was especially tense. I was thinking about all the work I needed to finish that day, and the short amount of time I had to do it. I was shorter than usual with my family and as everyone headed out, I finally, with a sigh, pulled out a stack of journals and notebooks and sat down at my dining room table.

My husband, perplexed, asked what I was up to. Curtly, I told him I needed to journal.

"I thought you needed to work," he offered, more matter-of-factly than I probably received it at the time.

"I DO! But I have to do all my journaling every day so that I can get everything done," I said, with the irony of what I was saying starting to click.

He gave me a look that said he was really trying to bite his tongue, and then managed to say, "You mentioned you don't have much time to get your work done today, and journaling takes time, yes?"

It was infuriating. How dare he mansplain my "me" time with my journals. And yet, as that stack of notebooks and guided written meditations weighed heavily next to me, I knew he had a point.

One of the aspirational phrases I wrote each and every day was: I am an efficient worker, who stays on task and is able to complete my work quickly.

I was literally writing that out every day, and yet here I was with a quiet house for a very limited amount of time. I could either muse about how I *wanted* to be that efficient worker, or I could actually *be* that person. All the journaling in the world could not meet my looming magazine article deadline. Only I could do that.

This is no diss on guided journaling and free writing. What I've learned about myself in the process of taking the regular time to reflect is valuable. I keep every journal and notebook that contains my personal thoughts. At this point, I need a small storage unit for them. I like to look back at how far I've come, or how my opinions and perspectives have evolved. It's interesting to see how the "me" who wrote those things has followed through, missed the mark, or simply changed her mind. Journaling is a healthy way to validate yourself and your feelings, allowing space to reconnect and reflect.

But journaling is also a form of escapism. I don't mean that in a derogatory way. At its foundation, journaling removes you from what is happening "in the moment" so you can reflect or plan. But the writing down of all the things, while incredibly insightful and helpful, should never be confused with the *doing* of the things. Just as we've already discussed at length in this book: Everything we *do* takes time and energy. Journaling and goal-setting is one of those areas. The time you take to write down your thoughts is finite. At some point, *you have to take what's on the paper and move it forward into an actionable state.*

This is true of any sort of thought or task strategizing. A grocery list is not very helpful if we take the time to create it, but never actually buy what we've listed. A to-do list is only worth something in the end if what we've outlined is accomplished. The same is true for the lists we make for our lives, goals, and legacy. Getting real with ourselves on paper (or screen) is integral to knowing where we want to go next, and in the future. But our collection of thoughts and words is the basis for our strategy; action is needed to move forward.

Move Forward

This may seem like a pretty shallow observation from someone who has already asked a lot of your time to read this book and complete the exercises. I stand by what we've accomplished together so far in this book—and I hope that you feel closer to your true calling and legacy as a result. But the *time has come* to take what we've analyzed, written, and crossed off and put all that into an actionable plan.

Action is scary sometimes. There's a meme I see floating around every few months on my social feed that says: "Start before you are ready." Another one that my algorithms feed me a lot says: "If you weren't ready, you wouldn't have the opportunity." Both statements require a great deal of action from the individual. It requires moving forward without having a guaranteed ending. It means that all of the goals we've written down may not come to fruition and our action will reveal to us which ones did (and didn't). These statements compel us to move forward, despite the outcome.

Ideally, we would all be repaid with dividends for our courage and ability to act. We would all be able to look back someday in the future and agree that the risks we took—the steps we took without a guaranteed outcome—were a monumental success. That's not always the case though. Bravery isn't always met with instant or straightforward success. Neither is audacity or action. But by taking the steps, by starting the thing, by making our own opportunities, we have a much better chance of building the life and outcomes of our dreams.

So that's where we stand right now in our Legacy List process. We are at the point where it's time to take action. And by taking action, of course I mean journaling and free-writing some more first and *then* taking the action. All of the work you've put in so far through the exercises in this book have brought you to this point, and I'm going to help you take all of those writings and turn them into actionable steps. I know you can do this. To quote another oft-shared meme, via the words of basketball great Michael Jordan: "You miss 100 percent of the shots you don't take."

It's time to take a shot (*Hamilton* fans, I know you feel me)—let's dive into our six-month action plan.

Exercise: Create a Six-Month Plan

Understanding your legacy can feel both empowering and overwhelming. I can't speak for you, but when I saw my own Legacy List laid out in front of me, I wanted to get started right away. But where did it make the most sense to start? And how would I get to the end goal—building my legacy—with all these other obstacles in my path? I did not find that I lacked motivation; the opposite was true. I lacked a clear-cut structure to get me to my goals.

And that's because there really isn't a clear-cut structure to ensuring your Legacy List is executed exactly like you envision it. There is never a straight path to achieving anything in life, and that's because there are just too many variables that we cannot foresee. I can guarantee you that what you envision for your Legacy List today will evolve with time, as you yourself grow and learn more about what chasing your legacy with focus looks like.

You may not be able to control the exact moments in your life but you can set forth with determination. And that starts with a plan to follow.

In this exercise, we're going to create a six-month plan to jump-start your Legacy List. This plan includes the action steps you will take, the assumed obstacles, and what you hope changes in that span of time. I'm sure you've heard the phrase, or seen the meme, that says something to the effect of: "A lot can change in a year." That is definitely true. But it doesn't take a year to see significant change. It can happen in months or weeks or even days. In this case, we're looking to enact some change in half a year.

I made my own six-month plan when I started this journey and update it as I go. It feels like just enough time to feel a difference in your life and also hold yourself accountable for an extended period of time.

Be sure that you have your other notes handy, especially the Legacy List we wrote in the last chapter. You'll want to reference them all as we begin to take our goals and place them next to actions. As we've done in past exercises in this book, try not to box yourself in. Yes, we'll identify some obstacles on our path to realistic change, but try to keep your dreams big as we work through this exercise.

Time to Write It Down

Let's get started on this six-month plan to jump-start your Legacy List.

1. Start by getting to a new page in your notebook, or the next space in your digital note or file. Label it as "My Six-Month Legacy List Plan" and write today's date. Next to today's date, write in the date that is six months from now.

2. Look at your Legacy List and determine an overarching change you'd like to see in six months' time. This will be a little more ambitious in nature. For example, if you want to enact change in your community, you may write something like: "In six months, I will feel vindicated that the work I'm doing is already making an impact." You can write a few statements like this that are more about the feelings you will have at the end of these first six months.

3. From there, start to write your action steps. Remember back in Chapter 2 when I talked about clearing your proverbial plate before adding more to it? That's what this step is all about. We need to start by deciding what things have to go in order to bring forth the new things you want to add. Write down at least three things you will change through elimination, or reduction, in the next six months and when. This will be tangible in nature. Here is the way I structure these for myself:

   Change Item: I will start going to bed an hour earlier so I can wake up an hour earlier to work on my Legacy List goals.

   Why: I want to designate quiet time before the day begins when I can work toward change, without the interruptions that happen once the day really gets started.

   When: I will start my new sleep schedule by this Sunday evening, October 10.

   Change Item: I will not take on the lead volunteer role for my church's holiday event this coming year.

   Why: I have done a great job setting this event up for success, and it is time to pass it off to someone new who can infuse it with new ideas, and free up my time for my Legacy List.

When: I will let the event coordinator know via email by Monday, October 11.

Change Item: I will restructure my appointments and errands to be concentrated to one day per week.

Why: Scheduling my errands and appointments in a central way will allow larger blocks of time to keep working on my Legacy List aspirations.

When: I will look at my monthly schedule and pick a day of the week for these items by Sunday, October 10. I will work to make it a reality no later than Monday, November 1.

As you begin to write these statements, you may find yourself writing more than three. This is completely fine, but remember that you do not want to overwhelm yourself. Real change takes time to enact, and you will get further by making a few clear, strong choices that you stick with than 10 that are impossible to execute. Have a lot of changes that you really want to get down on paper or screen? I suggest writing them all out and then going back through to prioritize them—starting with the three most important, or possible, in the first six months.

You can revisit this change list over time and keep knocking things off the list.

4. Decide how you will use your freed-up time to begin building your Legacy List. You may find that the "extra" time you have is only a few minutes per day, or even week. Never underestimate the power of what a little bit of time can do. It's why all the little things we commit to add up to so much time and effort—and also why giving focus to the right things, even in small amounts, can really stack up. Come up with at least three very specific goals that you want to chase in the next six months. Those high-in-the-sky dreams are important, but this exercise is about starting small. I'll share a few examples that may work for you, depending on what goals you want to reach. If a big goal on your Legacy List is to raise awareness for a cause that is close to your heart, you may have these three specific six-month goals:

   Goal: Continue to educate myself on this cause, including 20 minutes of research or reading about it every day.

   When: Start this Sunday, October 10.

   Goal: Create a list of people I know who can help me reach this goal and either meet with them in person, or create an email or text that explains why I'm investing my time in this cause and how I hope they can help me.

When: Start this list the week of October 10 and begin reaching out by November 1.

Goal: Develop a strategic plan to get my community more involved with my cause. This will include event, networking, and fundraising ideas.

When: Start drafting this plan by October 17 and have it solidified by December 17. Begin looking for ways to execute items on the plan by January 10. If a big goal on your Legacy List is to begin saving more money to reach financial goals like a new home or more vacations with your loved ones, you may have three specific six-month goals like these:

Goal: Speak with an accountant or wealth manager to start my savings plan.

When: Research or ask around about the best connections for this and make an appointment by October 17.

Goal: Enact the advice received on saving money, whether that is a separate account or simply saving more each time I'm paid.

When: Within two weeks of my meeting.

Create a separate savings account for my long-term financial goals.

Goal: Pick one thing to stop spending money on each week or month, and then consistently stick with it.

When: Decide by October 10 and eliminate it within one month.

If a big goal on your Legacy List is to be an even more invested parent or grandparent, you may have these three specific six-month goals:

Goal: Have at least one meaningful, five-minute conversation with each of my kids each day.

When: Start with just one kid per day for three weeks, and establish it as an everyday habit for all by November 1.

Goal: Take an active role in the activities my kids are participating in by volunteering in a small way for one item each.

When: Add one volunteer activity per month until each kid is covered.

Goal: Actively look for positive feedback for each of my kids.

When: Start by proactively saying something positive to each kid each day right away.

5. Decide what you want the six-month outcome to be for these goals and timelines. There are a few ways to determine this, but you can start with some statements that should trigger the way it feels. You can fill in these blanks:

   At the end of six months, I will feel more connected to my Legacy List if I ______________ .

   By ______________ , I will be establishing my Legacy List goal of ______________________ .

   When I actively commit to my Legacy List goals for six months, I will feel _________________ .

6. Schedule a time each week to look over these six-month goals and assess your progress. You may find that you need to tweak some, or set a new goal for others. The point is to not simply write these down and tuck them away in your notebook or device. You should be revisiting these, looking for ways to recommit to yourself over these first six months and keep all of the work we've done so far in this book close to your heart.

7. Schedule a date six months into the future when you will revisit these goals and set new ones—essentially raising the bar for yourself.

It's important that you pay attention to what is working and what is not. Remember, though, that these beginning months of building your Legacy List is more about alignment, and less about giant wins. At the end of six months you *will* see progress, even if it is not as huge or life-changing as you eventually hope to achieve.

Your mind, body, and spirit first need alignment with your new goals—they need to rewire themselves to meet your new self. This takes some undoing and may sometimes feel like a two-steps-forward-one-step-back plan. But those gains of just one step, or even half a step, do bring you closer to the version of you that wants to leave the most behind for this world. A six-month plan is a commitment to living these values more vividly and watching your path align as you go.

8

REALIGNMENT IS THE SECRET INGREDIENT

Aligning your path to your Legacy List has a funny way of showing you that you're on track. Your life may not change overnight, but when you are living in alignment with your calling, you start to see signs that you're going the right direction. Sometimes these signs are small, but pay attention to them. Soak in every positive wink from the universe as you continue on your path.

After I set to work on my life audit, I decided quickly that performing arts needed more than a side-gig place in my life. It popped up in every exercise I completed and was part of every journal entry I'd ever made. I knew that it was time to do what I said I would—take action on my calling. I knew I couldn't quit my full-time job as an online newsletter editor, or uproot my family to move to New York City as a 38-year-old wannabe Broadway star.

But where I was as a performer at that time was not where I really wanted to be. I knew I needed to start smaller and close to home—and that performing was accessible to me already, right where I was planted.

The easiest place to begin dreaming up my performing comeback, hot pink gel pen in hand, was my journal where I regularly wrote aspirational phrases about myself and who I hoped to become. I started writing this phrase on a daily basis: ***"I am a paid performer."***

I wasn't, which is the aspirational part of the exercise. I was writing the things I wanted to be, not the things that I actually was in my current stage of life. A paid performer was definitely an aspiration—at the time I wasn't even being asked to perform anywhere for free. But I had faith as I pressed that gel pen to the paper, day after day. I was going to write it enough times that it etched itself in my heart and brain, helping me discover the path toward making it a reality.

But let me take several steps back for a minute. This paid performer aspiration was a throwback in my life. A paid performer is what I originally set out "to be" as a young person. I attended college with the goal of earning a Musical Theatre degree and was accepted to one of the only true programs in my state at the time. I wanted to give singing, acting, and dancing for a living the triple-threat try.

I was already pretty skilled as an actress and vocalist, but the dancing was, well, lacking. I enthusiastically signed up for as many dance credits as I could feasibly have on my schedule: tap, jazz, contemporary. I even signed up for a beginner ballet course. I wanted to get better at that part. I knew it would hurt my chances of being cast anywhere professionally if my dancing wasn't at least passing. And that work, though painstaking at time, did help me improve my dance skills while I was in college.

What I didn't count on was how difficult it would be to stand out as an actress and singer. I had been one of the top people at both talents in high school, and never heard a "no" at an audition. Heck, I even got a "yes" within a few days of my audition to be in the program at my college. So imagine my surprise when, after my first round of college auditions for shows being produced on campus, I was not cast in anything. And not just *not* cast, I was not asked to read or sing anything extra, or come to any callbacks. I had not stood out to anyone. Not one director or student stage manager or anyone.

Devastation

I was devastated. What I now see as a normal part of the path to becoming a paid performer (rejection), in my 19-year-old head, it was a sign that I was not good enough to make it. I volunteered to help stage manage a few productions that year and kept going to my acting, singing, and dancing classes feeling like the bottom of an overstuffed barrel. I took the rejection personally, instead of as a normal part of the profession I was trying to make my career. achieve.

My closest friends were majors in other fields, and neither of my parents were performers. I didn't have an Instagram or TikTok algorithm to show me videos of how other people in my shoes had "failed and restarted" to see eventual success. I didn't have the wealth of life experience that showed me rejection can be the greatest teacher of all—and that a "no" might just mean a "no right now."

The casting story repeated itself my sophomore year, with a slight difference in the trajectory. After the August rounds of auditions, I was actually asked to come to a callback reading for the Greek classic *Lysistrata,* being directed by a visiting professor. My excitement at seeing my name on that callback sheet quickly spiraled into self doubt and fear. The thing I had wanted so badly for over a year—just the opportunity to vie for a role—had arrived. But instead of seizing this golden opportunity, I somehow managed to talk myself completely out of going to the callback at all. And that act of self-rejection, or self-sabotage, cut the deepest. If I didn't believe in myself, how would I ever manage to get anyone else to believe in me?

No one seemed to notice that I was missing from the callback and the cast list went up without my face on it.

I applied to student-direct a black box show that spring and was given that opportunity. I cast two women-centered one-acts later that fall and got to work on the nitty-gritty of character development with the cast. I quickly learned that I was good at directing, at building the right team to tell a story effectively. I was great at it, actually. I felt pride in what all of us collectively created for our audiences. The plays were quirky and strange and unsettling—exactly what you'd expect from a college-student director in charge of a show being held in the basement of the theatre building. It was glorious.

About a week after those one-acts closed, I had a scheduled meeting with my department mentor. This was a person assigned to me on Day One of college who had to check in with me twice a year or so, making this our third or fourth in-person meeting. His lore was that he was a former Los Angeles-based actor with lots of extra credits to his name. That made him an expert, I guess, on how the next generation could break into the biz.

Every meeting prior had been pretty uneventful. He had half-heartedly looked over my schedule and asked me a few questions about how it was going and that was it. Voila. Just a box checked by both of us so we could get back to whatever we had been doing before the meeting.

So, I wasn't expecting much when I went in to meet with him toward the end of my sophomore year in college. I had noticed him in the audience of my one-acts (probably just another box he needed to check as faculty), and I wondered fleetingly if he would mention it or give me the accolades I'd already heard from several professors and classmates. Maybe he'd tell me how much he enjoyed my directing style, how there was a real future for me leading casts and production crews, but that it was a shame I wasn't also on stage in the show. I wondered if he had finally noticed me, like, really noticed me, and would attempt more than small talk during our required meeting.

I entered his office and took a seat across from him. He was busily clicking through emails on his computer (with a noisy wired mouse), and I sat awkwardly as I waited for him to notice me. Eventually I must have caught the corner of his eye, because he turned away from the desktop computer to face me. He shuffled his papers around on a desk that looked eerily like mine does these days, stacked with unopened mail, theatre programs, and pen caps stuck between papers. From underneath a pile of flyers I recognized for a play that was performed the previous school year, he pulled out a flimsy, light pink flyer that had the name of my one-acts on the front. He opened it, as if to review exactly what he had seen, and flipped it over to read the thank yous on the back.

"I saw your plays," he started. I nodded at this fact.

"I've got to say, I really didn't get it," he continued, looking up at me for the first time.

Awkward silence.

"Get what?" I finally managed. "Do you mean the plot, or..."

He waved his hands in the air. "No, no. The plot was easy to follow. I didn't get the directorial choices."

It felt like the room heated up 10 degrees as he started to rattle off every single detail he didn't "get" about my directing as I sat across from him, dumbfounded. This went on for some time.

When he finally paused, I tried to remember everything every adult had ever told me about being a bigger person, and how to gracefully take criticism. Did I mention that I was only 19 years old?

"Art is subjective. You don't have to like the artistic choices I made," I managed, but he kept going. It's very possible he was making some valid points, ones that I could've taken into consideration for future projects. But I sat there, dumbfounded, feeling viscerally attacked. These performance pieces, my directorial debuts, were being stripped of their inherent value as I sat, blindsided, unable to defend them properly. I felt anger and shame and embarrassment, simultaneously. Worst of all, I felt guilt.

Had I let my performers down with my choices? Would the playwrights be disappointed in how I portrayed their beautiful and nuanced stories? When he finally wound down from his deconstruction of the performances, he paused and leaned forward on the desk to really drive home his next point.

"I'm worried about you, Katie. I don't think you are cut out for this industry."

My anger, shame, and embarrassment shifted quickly to a single feeling—despair.

After a year-plus of convincing myself that I didn't belong on the stage or screen, I had edited my dreams to fill my passion in a new way. Being handed the reins to create a production from scratch had lit something new inside me, something that felt real. I didn't know it at the time, but when I was at a rehearsal as a director, I was in a flow state. I lost all track of time, allowing myself to be fully immersed in the work we were doing. *Had I let my good feelings convince me that I was good at something that I clearly was not cut out to do? Was he right?*

By the end of that meeting, his feelings about my future were clear—he thought it was time to change my major and focus somewhere else. He had even taken the time to look over my transcript to determine that I had already earned a minor in Musical Theatre. It would be so easy to walk away now, with that minor, and not "lose" anything—or that was the implication screaming in my brain. I felt ambushed and alone.

By the end of the meeting, I was numb. Clutching the transcript with his circles and handwriting, I left my final meeting as a Musical Theatre major. The next week, I declared English as my new major and signed up for some summer courses in literature to try to catch up in my new field.

I share this story because this single meeting has replayed in my head in the decades since, with different words coming out of my mouth that defended my directorial decisions, my place in that theatre program, my dreams. I think we've all been there in our lives. And I realize it is all-too-easy to villainize another person in your narrative about the decisions you make in life, but I've tried to stop doing that. Because in truth, the path I took following that day has been a beautiful one, filled with journeys that brought me joy, a career, a spouse, children, and wonderful communities, both in person and online. Those 20 minutes of my young adult life don't define me, and neither should any one situation or circumstance in your life.

That meeting is part of my story, though. In an about-face way, it is part of my Legacy List that includes mentoring young performers and fighting for my life out here to stay a paid performer myself. And it taught me not to let one opinion, or even many, sway me from what I know to be my calling, carefully constructed and strengthened through the exercises in this book. And just a reminder—that temporal, decision-making lobe in our brains isn't fully formed until age 25. Sometimes we end up living with the decisions we make in those early years for a long time, but it's never too late to be what you could have been.

Praise at Last

Following my major change, to the outside world—my parents, my roommates, my theatre friends—I used the excuse that I changed majors because I wanted to be more employable (not really the smartest switch if that was the case). I was too embarrassed to admit that I clearly couldn't cut it. And I loved writing—I always had, and I always will. I was met in my new English-centric classes with praise from my professors who gave me the type of criticism that made me feel seen, not isolated. In red pen along the margin of a personal essay I wrote, the head of the English department (and my professor) wrote: "Katie, Your writing needs to be read. Keep up the good work."

And because I was young, and sad, I mistook praise for a universal sign that I had made the right choice. I took being immediately "good" at something as a reason to keep doing it. I let the opinion of one person completely change the course of my life.

And look. I absolutely love writing. I was a huge Carrie Bradshaw fan in the early 2000s, because, who wasn't? With each term paper I turned in and each essay I emailed to my professors, visions of sitting in my Manhattan brownstone and looking out my window at the bustling world below as I typed my latest important column for the world to read flooded my brain. And even when the reality of being a paid writer eventually set in—from the low-paying job of editing a pharmaceutical journal to sitting through utility board meetings at a small newspaper in Indiana—I still loved it. I was still good at it. At times, I was exceptional.

But it didn't take much to miss the creative side of performing and working behind the scenes. I stopped watching awards shows that I'd always loved, The Oscars and The Golden Globes, because my dreams of being there one day were gone. It was painful to see other people living that dream so fully. I declined offers to go see professional shows, and even community theatre. It wasn't until I was a parent myself, with little ones who showed propensity in the performing arts, that I started to even slightly let performing arts back into my brain. I could only go to a theatre and watch a musical if my kindergartener was a singing princess.

And as I watched my own little young people and their friends fall in love with the performing arts, I started to see through my pain for the first time. I started to feel the true heartbreak that I still harbored from what I had quit all those years before. But that insight met me, and left me, as a passing thought, mostly. My writing career and life as a parent kept me plenty busy. I had no room in my life for anything else, not even an unfulfilled dream.

It wasn't until my mom's Alzheimer's diagnosis that the small flickering wick of that dream fully ignited again. I knew I'd left it alone long enough. It was time to reclaim it, whatever shape that took in my life.

So to loop back to my post-epiphany journaling, I also knew writing the words "paid performer" in my private journal would never be enough to get the job done. Those writings were just to continue to inspire myself.

My next step was a different kind of journaling, or "live chronicling." I shared my desire to get back into the performing arts, specifically musical theatre, on my social media. Sometimes it was a direct ask for people to connect me to the right people or opportunities, and other times it meant hitting "follow" on accounts to help me get back in the game. I began to align at least part of my outside-facing identity with the life of a musical theatre performer, and to do it regularly.

And as much as I believe social media has some true reach that matters, I knew even that wasn't enough. I had to get out there and actually perform if I had any hope of getting paid for it one day.

Nothing but Blue Skies

During the final week of 2019, the year my mom was diagnosed with early-onset Alzheimer's disease and nine months into my own Legacy List creation, I made a New Year's resolution to perform in something in 2020. Again, this was the final week of 2019—nothing but blue skies on the horizon for my goal. Surely I could track down something to perform within the next calendar year. How hard could it be? Sure, I was a little out of practice. And I had no recent experience to speak of. But I was willing to say "yes." I was ready to stand in the back and sing as a tree, or be part of a chorus of some sort. I wasn't picky. I just knew I needed to be cast in *something* to feel like I was moving in the right direction. As the ball dropped on Times Square welcoming in 2020, and I sat in my living room with my kids and husband, I felt calm surrounding my goals for the first time since my mom's diagnosis. My intentions were set and I was willing to work for them. It was time to simply pay attention.

On the second day of 2020 I received a call from someone producing an Orlando International Fringe Festival show that involved Britney Spears' music. She asked if I wanted to join the cast and explained the role they had in mind for me. What I didn't know when I enthusiastically yelled "YES!" into the phone was that it was actually a paid gig. It wasn't much, just enough to cover gas for rehearsals for five months, but it was paid. I was handed money at the end of the project for my participation as Fit/Pregnant Brit, singing my face off with a fake belly to the song "Stronger."

Less than a week after writing down the goal of performing once in 2020, it had manifested, albeit interestingly due to the onset of the Covid pandemic. We ended up recording our show and selling virtual tickets to see it, but I was still paid and had a fresh performing credit to add to my sparse and outdated resume.

And despite the toll social distancing took on live art, I managed to perform in two other musical theatre productions in 2020. And I have performed every year since in at least one project.

Now, I wish I could tell you that simply writing it down and sharing it on social media was all it took to get the attention of that Fringe Festival producer. It wasn't. In fact, she was more interested in my superfan level admiration of Britney Spears and willingness to make "weird art" than my actual talent or potential. But I'd been planting the seeds of my paid performer aspiration for three-quarters of a year through my journaling, social media posts, and in-person conversations. And without doing at least those things, she wouldn't have had a clue I was even interested or had me on her radar.

Me a Teacher?

Through that gig I was asked to substitute for a voice teacher affiliated with that same organization who was off for maternity leave ("As way leads to way..."). I agreed to do so half-heartedly. I loved *being* a performer and was still recutting my teeth on it. But teaching others to perform? That wasn't for me. Being a teacher of any kind had never been on my list of professions that I wanted to do. Not as a kid or teen or college student. Certainly not as a mom-of-five pushing 40.

And yet, as I took on that reluctant first role ever as a teacher, at age 38, I was surprised at how much

I enjoyed it. It turns out that I actually had a lot of insight and wisdom to share with my pupils and some practical techniques as well. I looked forward to seeing my temporary students week after week and watching them progress in their disciplines. I even picked up a few students of my very own in the process—new people who signed up while my colleague was out of the office who then would stay with me when she returned, if I wanted to keep teaching them. I made more in a month filling in for that other teacher than I had in five months of rehearsing and performing the Fringe show.

I started to wonder: Could my goal of becoming a paid performer extend to being a paid *teacher* of performance?

Of course, they were two different areas of expertise, but on my path to finding the first, had I stumbled into a strong second? Was this a way to further immerse myself in a world that I loved and earn some money in the process?

I quickly found that teaching young people was like a crash course in everything new in musical theatre. The shows I had missed out on for the past 15 years were old knowledge to these kids. Of course, I loved introducing them to classics—musicals such as *Grease* and *Rent*—but I was soaking in the twisted tunes from *Ride the Cyclone,* and the stage adaptations of *Mean Girls* and *Legally Blonde* (movies I had loved as a young person, and musicals I realized I loved as a late-30-something person). Soon I knew every song from *Hamilton,* and *Six,* and *Hadestown.* Teaching my students was the fastest way to get myself back on track as a performer who had stepped away for a while.

When the teacher I was filling in for returned from her maternity leave, her students returned to her. I missed them. I found myself asking that teacher how they were doing and what songs they were working on. As new private voice students filtered into the studio, they were placed with her. I started to feel a little bit resentful. I knew the assignment; it was clear when I took it. I wasn't taking her job. I was filling in while she was out. And frankly, when I said yes to filling in, I was relieved that the gig was temporary. It wasn't until I actually *taught* that I realized how much I enjoyed it and how good I actually was at doing it.

My Own Space

I decided to start seeking my own private students outside the studio space. Nothing major, just a student here and there who I could work alongside to help them grow. I still had a full-time remote editing job, and was actively seeking performing opportunities of my own, but I had dipped my toe in the teaching waters and I knew I had to follow the pull of that riptide, at least a little further.

Within a year of that hesitant "yes" to being a substitute teacher, the momentum was carrying me forward. The more people I taught, and the more music I learned to teach to others, the more my own performing improved. I started to take my own advice on confidence in auditions, and letting myself make mistakes in pursuit of improvement. My music sightreading skills, which had been pretty strong as a 16 to 22 year old, came back slowly but surely. I felt the wisdom of every lesson learned while teaching when I entered my own auditions, rehearsals, and performances.

It felt different from the day I said a hesitant "yes" to filling in for someone. This felt like an empowered decision, one that I was fully choosing as part of my Legacy List path. I decided to stop moving slowly and in small ways. I knew it was time to be bold. I wanted to see how far this performing arts path would take me.

Everything moved pretty quickly from the day I decided to wholeheartedly seek out teaching opportunities. A handful of students started coming to my home for 30-minute lessons at my piano. My dogs would bark. And my kids would be warned to stay *out* of the room when I was teaching. But our house is small and the piano is in a common area. It was working, sort of, but I knew I needed a dedicated space for these students, even if it was just a few of them.

And that's when a friend reached out about a new space she was planning to rent near my home. She had some cool co-op space ideas and wondered what I thought about the area because it was so close to my home. After giving her the greenlight from a community perspective, I asked her if there was a chance I could rent some space from her. Just a room or a closet or even the lobby. Anywhere, really. She cut me a fantastic deal; and soon, I was teaching my handful of lessons from a quiet, dog-free space where no one called me "Mom." And since I had the space, I started to promote the fact that I was teaching a little more. Soon I had a few more students. And then a few more after that.

My teaching promos had caught the attention of a local theatre where I had performed in a recent production of *Evita.* I interviewed for a contract position as a music director for their upcoming season and was hired for two shows. As I served in that position in each show, more and more people asked me about the voice lessons I offered. The youth program director at that theatre asked me if I'd be interested in future opportunities for music directing there, too. She started sending my name as a reference when people asked for private voice lessons and my stable of students started to steadily grow. In a matter of six months, I went from teaching 3 hours per week to 15 hours.

Typing in the words "voice lessons" on my social media accounts triggered a series of advertisements based on my algorithms, too. Soon I was getting all sorts of offers to enroll and earn my Master of Fine Arts, or sign up for hyper-niche classes on running a performing arts business. I ignored them all for the most part. I was happy, slowly figuring it out as I went. Like I said, I ignored them...for the most part.

One especially persistent ad was for New York University's online certification, Performing Arts Industry Essentials. The program boasted access to NYU professors, Broadway performers, and the tools to make a career out of the performing arts—beyond simply performing. I finally took the clickbait and found myself down a rabbit hole, reading about the program and its benefits.

I signed up and paid nearly $1,000 for a certification program I wasn't even sure I needed. From a purely vain perspective, I hoped I could come in contact with a *real* Broadway star or producer in the process (spoiler alert: that did not happen). But from an academic perspective, I was excited to dive back into the subject I had long ago loved so dearly.

The mornings I blocked out time for my studies were glorious. I'd get my kids out the door to school, finish just enough "real work" to convince my bosses that I was indeed good at my job, and then cozy up with a fresh cup of coffee and my notebook. I devoured the video lessons, and got lost in the reading materials. I was pleasantly surprised to learn that not everything in the business of theatre had changed in the 20 years since I took similar classes in college.

Things like stage directions, and how to block a show, and what each role in a production meant were still the same. But the type of theatre being performed, the roles being offered, and the style of music being performed were all evolving, and quickly. The business of harnessing that into something marketable, and in demand, fascinated me. It was true that I was listening to example stories about some of the best in the business, but I started to wonder what it would be like to take my love of performing-turned-teaching to an even higher level. *What if I added entrepreneurship to that path? But where would I start...and what would it even look like?*

The next step in my teaching path knocked once before I felt ready to open the door. My friend reached out about the space she was leasing to me and said she was going to move on to other things. She wondered if I wanted to take over the lease. With the amazing deal I already had in front of me (via the very reasonable rent she charged me), and all of the "real life" things on my plate outside my side gig of teaching, I told her "no." I said I really didn't think I could take on the extra overhead and didn't have the additional time to expand my own offerings. She understood and said she'd just stick it out for the time being too.

I meant what I said when I told her "no." And she respected it. But what she didn't know was that her simple ask started a flurry of "what ifs" in my own head.

What if I *did* take over the space? What then? Was there more I could use it for? Would I be able to fill the space and hours with people who wanted to pay to be there? In a perfect world with no time or financial constraints, what could I achieve? And who could I ask to help me?

Four months came and went after her initial ask. I put up my two Christmas trees, and took them back down, and watched yet another ball drop in Times Square. It was four months of showing up to my small rented room and looking at the rest of the space through an entrepreneurial lens.

Thoughts swirled. Could we hold classes here, in addition to private lessons? Could we host summer camps? Maybe an open mic night, or even an entire musical or play? Overall, it wasn't much space—only around 1,100 square feet including two single-unit bathrooms. But it was nearly 10 times the size of my rented room within it—at about 4 times the cost.

I sat down and ran the math using a precious page of my journal to multiply and divide in bright gel pen colors. The numbers showed me something encouraging. If I kept up my current roster of students, I could break even each month. If I expanded my offerings, even slightly, I could actually make money. I looked at my calendar to see where I could add voice students and saw very few opportunities. I didn't see how I could even begin to add more to my plate.

But then I had another idea. What if instead of limiting what I offer to just myself and a very niche service, I opened it up to more offerings, more teachers and just *more* of everything?

All of the units I'd breezed through in my NYU program flooded my brain. The business of performing arts—was it a business I wanted to be in? And could I feasibly make it work?

I texted my friend—seemingly out of the blue to her, I'm sure—and told her I had a change of heart from four months prior. I wondered how much longer was on her lease and how quickly she would want to sign it over to me, if the offer still stood. She informed me that there were just four months left on her original lease and that she'd be happy to sign it over to me. We spoke with the landlord who was also fine with the arrangement.

I spoke to my husband about all of it because I like talking to him. Also, the overhead I commit to and the income I earn (or lose) affects him too. He and I walked away from the conversation of the same mind—a four-month lease was a low-risk way to give some of my many ideas a shot. If they all failed miserably, then we would simply not re-sign and I could decide what to do next.

But if my ideas showed potential, and if people showed up, then it may be worth investing another year of time via a renewed lease.

And since I was just giving it a try anyway, I figured, *Why hold back?*

Beachside Performing Arts

I immediately reached out to other performer and teacher friends to see what they wanted to contribute. I asked another friend to come on board as another private voice teacher. I found people willing to plan and teach an array of summer camps. My friend who had relinquished her space to me said that she'd be interested in teaching private lessons or classes. I gave the newly-imagined studio space a name—Beachside Performing Arts—along with the website and social media to go with it. I started promoting the *heck* out of everything and holding my breath to see what happened next.

By the end of those four months, my personal voice teaching schedule had doubled and my associate teacher had two full days of students. We hosted three summer camps and produced two musicals that summer—and created a sign-up for our fall classes. I spoke with my landlord and signed on the dotted line for another 12 months. Much like what happened when I made the decision to choose teaching performing arts (and not just hesitantly dipping my toe in it), when I signed that lease I felt like a fire had been lit under my feet. I was choosing this next step in the path, and I was determined to see it through.

Our fall classes filled up. I hired more private lesson teachers. We produced several more musicals. Just five months into my new entrepreneurial journey, a friend in the performing arts space reached out. She had her own performing arts school, about 35 minutes away from mine, that she had launched about a decade earlier. She had built a solid foundation of families and teachers but the time had come for her to step back from the business. She considered just closing her doors. But then she remembered seeing what I'd been posting on social media about my own studio and had an idea, what if she sold her business to me?

Another "what if"—for her, and for me.

When she first contacted me, my answer was "no." It was terrible timing. I was still trying to get my other studio location fully established, and the holiday season was on the way, and I *still* had a full-time job and five kids at home. I appreciated that she thought of me. But I politely declined.

And gosh darn it, if it wasn't five minutes later that my brain started to swirl again. Two locations? Could that even be something within my realm of possibility? Could I actually pull off two new locations within nine months' time? Would my teachers and staff be willing to help me? Would my friend's current staff at her location stay? Could I afford to *buy* the business, staff it, and pay overhead—while maintaining my other location too?

My husband bit his tongue when I told him about what my friend had offered. He could see my bubbling excitement trying to seep out from the nonchalant delivery of the story. He could tell that I wanted to do it, to take the next step in my fast-flowing path. He reminded me that if she simply closed her doors, most of her students would likely migrate my way anyway. And he had a point.

But I wondered about the students who would simply stop their journey instead? The ones who lived too far for their parents to drive them to lessons at our other location. The ones who were barely finding the time for classes already—and who would take an indefinite break from it if their home studio closed. I thought about what my business model should shift to if we expanded. And I signed the dotted line before Christmas.

As another ball dropped in Times Square, I thought about all that had transpired on my Legacy List path and the leaps that had been taken since I first reluctantly said "yes" to substituting a few voice lessons—a gig that crossed my path as I doggedly pursued that "paid performer" ambition on my Legacy List.

It was not lost on me that in less than a year, I had gone from teaching in a 10' by 10' space to leasing an entire office unit—and was considering the addition of another one. My staff had gone from one (me) to seven, and if I added this second location that number would jump to 15. I had gone from a very part-time voice teacher to a business owner, producer, and business prospector, apparently. My performing arts empire was practically building itself in front of my very own eyes. And I was incredibly grateful.

My path to teaching performing arts, and enabling others to do the same, wasn't written expressly on my Legacy List. But as I started to meticulously seek out the dreams that *were* on those lists, the teaching component emerged. That's what happens when you are aligned; the parts of your Legacy List that are supposed to arise do. And they don't feel like the obligations that weigh you down. These feel like an energy boost, a ray of sunshine, a whisper of hope.

There's a fine line, of course, between distractions and life clutter and signs that you are supposed to shift your direction. Don't be afraid to reaudit, reassess, and rewrite your Legacy List as you go.

Exercise: Audit and Reassess

Great American poet Robert Frost put it so eloquently in his poem *The Road Not Taken* when he wrote: "Yet knowing how way leads on to way, I doubted if I should ever come back." It's not the most popular part of the poem, or the section that is most quoted. But even as a young person, it was always the part of the poem that spoke most to me. Our paths are always moving forward and even if we have the best intentions, we can never truly go back to a place, or a moment in time. It's always slightly, or overtly, different when we do. That line has always struck me as profoundly beautiful because of its simple truth—way leads on to way.

Earlier in the poem, Frost mentions that when the two paths diverged in front of him, he could save one of them for another day (I'm paraphrasing) if he chose to return. But as the course of the poem continues, it becomes clear that those two specific paths will never present themselves again. Two new paths might—but those two choices, in what I always imagined was a warm, fall light with burnt orange foliage in the background—would never show up again. Not in the same way. Not in the same light.

We can apply this idea to our Legacy Lists. Way leads onto way. As we align ourselves with the calling of our lives, with what we truly feel driven to accomplish, we will come to new divergences. We will see new scenery, or perhaps familiar scenery in a new light. What might have sounded lofty and romantic when we first audited our lives and wrote draft number one of our Legacy List may transform into something completely different. We might have to start over.

Or, we may find that all of the hard work we did in creating and beginning to execute our Legacy List was right as it should be—but needs a little editing to truly reach its full potential.

Whatever the case, revisiting your Legacy List is an important part of fulfilling it.

One way to do this is to simply start at the beginning, with the exercise from Chapter 1 and edit the points in the process that you want to adapt. I revisit mine regularly—sometimes every few months.

If you don't want to do all of that, or want to create more of a litmus test to determine what steps to take next, you can answer the following questions. This can help guide you to what your next movement should be and if you need to edit or realign any of your Legacy List aspirations.

You can redo your full list or answer these questions at any point in the process (and by "process" I mean living your life in an aligned way). It's important to stay committed to what you've uncovered about yourself, but not to tether yourself to goals and values that feel misaligned. The following questions are designed to help you determine what feelings may be grounded in negative emotions, and which ones are true intuitions that you should heed.

When It's Time to Write It Down...

Answer these questions to reassess your Legacy List:

- Despite challenges, do I still feel fiercely aligned with the daily actions I'm taking to build my Legacy List?
- What is the biggest obstacle in my way right now?
- What or who is stressing me out?

- Do I feel less invested in any part of my Legacy List than I did at the start? What has changed to make me feel that way?
- If no one was watching, or knew any of the Legacy List work I am doing, what would I change?
- What impact have I already made by leaning into my Legacy List?
- Am I reacting to outside forces or influences, or do I feel inside myself that I need to make a change?

From these questions and answers, a clearer perspective should start to emerge that will help you decide where to edit, and where to double down.

9

WHEN LIFE THROWS YOU OFF COURSE

Setting your Legacy List intentions is wildly important to ensuring that you clear the path in front of you. Creating our intentions, revisiting our "why," upholding our time and resource boundaries, and listening to our intuition as we go are all ways we can ensure a legacy that will outlive us. Not everything will go our way, however. There are going to be setbacks and maybe even some heartbreak as your Legacy List unfolds. It won't always feel good, either. There will be days when you wonder how you will ever reach the next pinnacle, and days when it feels easier to just conform to the hustle and bustle of the world around you rather than blazing your own trail.

I know because I'm living my Legacy List. There are days when I feel discouraged and days when my feelings are hurt. There are days when the success of everything I'm doing also feels heavy—like the more I succeed, the heavier the pressure. But in case no one has ever told you this before, it is completely normal to feel overwhelmed by your sheer power and potential. Yes, it is empowering to imagine all that we can create and change but it can also feel overwhelming. That is because we, as human beings, are so talented, so brimming with opportunity, that our own greatness can overwhelm us.

I've also found that the more I lean into my Legacy List, the more urgency I feel. There is nothing wrong with ambition and drive, but there are days when I have to remind myself that each step is still a step. Not every day or week or month or year is a sprint; some are slower strides that still move us forward, allowing us the rest and perspective we need to absorb for the next step.

I am telling you all of this because I want you to be prepared. I want you to be so sure of yourself and of your Legacy List that even the worst days or experiences won't throw you permanently off course. You may declare your intentions only to find roadblock after roadblock on your path. A cynic may say that this is your sign to abandon your Legacy List and its components. But I say it just means it's time to look for another way.

If you have done all of the exercises in this book and read up to this point and feel secure about the aspirations on your Legacy List, then there's no need to look for "signs" from the universe to stop. It just means to look for new ways to set your course. There is more than one way to build a positive life that will outlive you. But you won't find that blissful little side street if you give up your journey when the most obvious road is blocked.

We all have stories of defeat and heartbreak in our past. Some we never truly move past but they are all part of who we are today, in this moment. I've had my share of them, including my mom's diagnosis, which I've discussed in this book. I was also a single mom for a few years in my 20s. I've been evicted from an apartment (with a baby in tow), and I've had a car repossessed. My husband and I accepted public assistance for a short period when we first married, and couldn't figure out how to make our family work and still earn enough money to feed said family. I've lost friends and family to disease and accidents and the throes of addiction. The point is: I've experienced setbacks and some downright unfair things that have happened to me in my life. And those things will continue, God willing sparingly, even as I'm building and living my Legacy List.

A Keener Sense of Life

But the difference in my life now is that in trying to understand my legacy, I have developed a keener sense of the human experience. I don't have any reasonable expectations of smooth sailing, health, longevity, cognizance or "happiness," whatever that looks like. I know that my life is temporary and my trials are a drop in the bucket compared to the world's suffering.

But I also know that my life, and what I choose to do with it, is important. Every moment of every day presents another opportunity for me to grow past my current constraints and level up my legacy.

Though the experiences I listed—eviction and repossession—likely caught your eye, let me tell you a milder story about a setback I faced while on this Legacy List journey. The difference between the laundry list of challenges and this one is that the example I'm about to share happened while I was actively working on my Legacy List. In fact, the ramifications are so raw that it still bothers me on a nearly daily basis. I thought about *not* writing about it for that reason; I don't have perspective on it yet. I don't yet know what lessons it will teach me in 10 or 20 years.

But we don't have to fully reconcile the "lesson" of our obstacles for them to still be teaching us now. And maybe my sharing of this will help you as you navigate the rough patches of your own Legacy List.

A Lesson Still Learning

Remember earlier in the book when I told you the story about how I transitioned from performer-only to performer-teacher (and then entrepreneur)? I was so excited about moving my legacy forward and leaning into the momentum of my journey that I made a few missteps. I can't even blame my Legacy List for them, either. I used that as an excuse to let narcissism and people-pleasing take over.

When I interviewed to music direct the main-stage adult shows at the theatre I mentioned earlier, I had never taken on such a role. I'd helped with youth music at the studio where I originally started teaching voice lessons, but I had never been handed the musical score to an entire production and been told to teach it to a room of professionals. This wasn't something I hid. In my interview, I mentioned assistant music directing to start, or doing some of the smaller shows first, while I got my bearings. I can read and play music on the piano, and understand part-singing just fine. And I've been in enough productions to know how to run a music rehearsal. But I knew I probably needed a warmup option—a way to dip my toe, like I'd done before, and then feel more comfortable taking a leadership role.

Imagine my surprise when three weeks later I received a call offering me the full role of music director for two of the shows. I immediately felt my stomach clench, as if it was releasing 1,000 butterflies into my throat. But it just felt so good to be picked for something, and this early into my Legacy List journey, that I immediately accepted what felt like a monumental task. Times two.

Besides, I had months to prepare for both. And I knew *how* to play notes and sing them.

But still. Immediately my anxiety kicked in. I woke up a few nights in a sweat, thinking about notes on the page. My music wasn't immediately available to me, so I tried finding it other places so I could get a headstart. I worried that everyone would immediately spot me as a fraud, as an imposter. And yes, I use that word purposefully because I was, in fact, displaying traits of imposter syndrome. But I was also just not ready.

I didn't want to admit that at the time, and it's hard to say even now. But it's true. The feelings of inadequacy I was feeling were based on reality. It was true that I didn't have the experience or skill level—yet—to take on those tasks.

I could have politely turned down the offer. I could have been honest about my capabilities. Heck, I could've lied about why I was turning it down. There are times when anxiety lies to you—but this was a time it was trying to protect me.

I didn't let it though. I was too bowled over by the idea of being at the heart of the theatre magic and too flattered by being asked to join the inner circle. I liked being picked for something that felt like a step up in my newly aligned performing path. I had not agreed to this role because it matched up with my Legacy List goals of improving as a performer and providing opportunities for others. I had accepted it because it feels good to land a part. That's just the honest truth, especially in an industry like performing. I found solace in Instagram memes that said things such as "Start before you're ready." I wasn't ready, but I was starting. And that's what I was supposed to do, right?

And look, it wasn't all bad. In fact, I think I did a pretty good job ensuring the cast had what they needed to perform their very best. If any members of that cast or crew read this book, they'll likely reach out to me to tell me what a great job I did and how they would love to work with me again. And that's really kind of them.

But I was inexperienced and it showed. A few months later when I music directed the second of the shows I was contracted for, it really showed. I received my music just three days before rehearsal started, and I was out of town at the time. I showed up to the first music rehearsal unprepared, and did my best to just play and teach on the spot. I wasn't fooling anyone.

When the second show of the contract ended, I didn't feel accomplished or proud (of myself). I just felt relieved. And despite all those months of anxiety, the hours in the rehearsal room feeling unworthy and the weight that felt like it was lifted when it was all done, I put my name in to do it again for the following season. I'd learned some lessons since the year before and I felt like I could do it again, but better.

Imagine my surprise when my colleagues started receiving their contracts for the next season and I heard nothing. Not an email. Not a text. Not a call. Nothing.

I waited a few days after the initial contracts were offered and reached out to the theatre. I was told offers were still being made. So I waited. And in the waiting, I was able to piece together the shows that others were offered and with each excited friend's text reply, my heart sank a little more. They weren't going to ask me back, at least not to music direct.

Feelings of embarrassment flooded my senses as I took a stupid walk for my stupid mental health. They weren't going to pick me. What would my friends who were picked think? Would word get back to the students at my studio and would it hurt my business? What were people saying about me? In pursuing my Legacy List, or at least feigning that pursuit, had I actually set myself back? In "starting before I was ready," did I ruin future opportunities?

And I think we've all been there. We've all heard a "yes" or a "no" when we didn't expect it. In this case, I heard both at different times for the same position.

You'd think that the enlightened version of myself on the path to building my Legacy List would have shrugged this off. *Que sera sera,* or something like that. But when I tell you that I had a hard time with it, dear reader, I really struggled for a while. I toggled between embarrassment and anger and resentment.

I talked to my husband and closest friends about it, admitting that I knew I shouldn't be taking it so personally or hard. They listened like the wonderful angels they all are and then all said something similar: "This means you'll have more time for *your* performing arts projects." Like my burgeoning studio. And my own performing endeavors. They were right and I knew it. But it hurt to be rejected.

I wondered aloud to my husband if maybe my dreams just needed to take a backseat. Why couldn't I just work at my normal full-time job and get off at a normal time like a normal person? My legacy pursuit was just adding hours to my days, and stealing my sleep, and making everything more difficult. Plus, my feelings were getting hurt more than if I never tried anything at all risky.

Why did I have dreams? Why did I feel a calling so urgently? Why couldn't I just be numb and simple?

But as I was bemoaning this relatively trivial thing that had happened on my path, the flowers were blooming all around me. My studio was bursting at the seams. My personal voice lesson schedule was full, with a waitlist. Within months, I'd end up purchasing another performing arts business. A few months after that I signed a contract for my first book. All while my kids were continuing to grow up happy and healthy, beginning to pursue their own paths.

The time I would have spent agonizing over every music note, or lying awake wondering how many wrong notes I was inevitably going to play in front of a room of performers, went to answering business inquiry emails and producing our own shows within our studio. I was no longer scared to play or sing in front of a room of people there to learn from me and got stronger with each production, class and lesson that I touched. The rejection started to feel more like a blessing, and less of a slight. And even if it was a slight—I was beginning to care less and less.

Trial and Error and Success

Our Legacy List is what we hope to accomplish, but there is no exact manual to getting there. As we keep trying new things and going on new excursions, there are going to be setbacks and roadblocks and heartbreaks and days when we feel inadequate, unworthy, and even like an imposter. But if you are aligning your actions with that core list, with those "whys," then nothing you do on the path will be wasted. You'll leave the impact you hope to leave.

It's important to recognize the actions and components that are in our control, and the ones that truly aren't.

We *can* control our perspective and the individual steps we take to strengthen our list. We *can* control our attitude toward change and challenges. We *can* set and maintain our boundaries.

We *cannot* control the opportunities people are not willing to extend to us. We *cannot* control the way people respond to our attitude or boundaries. We *cannot* control how people feel about us or our dreams.

And once we acknowledge the difference between what we can control and what we simply must let go—we can breathe a little easier.

And at the end of it all, we will not be able to control the stories that are told about us. I could quote *Hamilton* again here, but the real ones know what I'd say here if I were to do so. We only have control over the pebble in our hand at any given moment that we dare to propel forward onto still water, watching the ripple effect until it is beyond our viewpoint.

We cannot control that ripple—only the velocity and strength of the toss. If we're lucky, it will travel the way we intended, making beautiful, connected arcs along the way. If we're really lucky, our intended path will stray a little from what we planned, showing us even bigger and more beautiful arcs as the pebble travels.

Exercise: Imagine the Hard Days and Strategize Next Steps

I think I've made it clear in this chapter that hard days are inevitable, even when you are aligned with your path. That's not cynicism speaking because I am not saying that you cannot weather those hard times. You can. And will. But I won't be there to remind you of your strength in those moments. You may have close friends or loved ones who are willing to remind you, if you are blessed. But no matter what your support situation, you will always have yourself to remind you what you need to do next.

It's not gloom and doom to envision difficulties. It's realistic. It helps us confront fears of what could happen with a plan, or at least form an awareness around it.

Let me loop back to a challenge I mentioned earlier in this chapter—single parenting my first child for three years (and during my pregnancy, too). When I was 24, I found out that I was unexpectedly pregnant. For reasons that were out of my control, the father immediately removed himself from the scenario. I knew from the day that I found out I was pregnant that I would have to walk the path to parenthood alone, should I choose it.

I struggled with what to do next, tossing and turning alone in bed each night, dealing with the constant heartburn that had already kicked in. I had only moved to Florida a few months prior, leaving all my family and friends over 1,200 miles away. It was convenient in a way. I didn't have to see any of them as I allowed myself to internally struggle, keeping quiet about my situation for what felt like eternity, but was in reality more like three or four weeks.

Eventually I blurted it out to Mom on an afternoon call between my newspaper job and my waitressing job. She asked me, cautiously, how I felt about it. I apologized for finding myself in that predicament, telling her I know it must feel very disappointing on her end and that it was likely not part of her and my dad's plan for me.

My mom, a woman of staunch faith, replied, "God doesn't care about our plans. Only His." And other than checking on how I was feeling and asking if I was eating and sleeping enough, my mom gave me the space to continue processing what my brain and body was going through. It wasn't until I was through my first trimester when I absentmindedly mentioned something about "when the baby comes" that she quietly asked through the phone, "Oh, is the baby going to come?" And it occurred to me that I had made the decision to continue the path to motherhood, but I had neglected to tell my mom that news.

I replied, "Yes, I'm sure I'm going to do everything I can to make sure he or she gets here safely." And I heard the loudest sigh on the other end of the line—accompanied by what sounded like sobbing. When she regained her composure, Mom said, "Oh I'm just so happy. I've been on my knees every night praying for my grandchild."

It's all about perspective. What I was viewing as a complication, as a pretty big roadblock in my life, was being viewed as a blessing by someone else. I know everybody loves a baby, but the parents (or parent) actually have to raise that baby. Debating that responsibility and the choices people make surrounding it would be an entirely different book; and frankly, I don't want to write it. But sometimes it takes pause, or maybe even outside encouragement, to reframe our struggles as opportunities. My mom's joy through the phone that day reminded me that low moments are just that—moments. We can build from the ground up over and over again in our lives to create a life that's truly breathtaking.

During that pregnancy, I remember people telling me over and over again how incredibly difficult being a parent was going to be—particularly doing it on my own. Most didn't offer advice, just warnings. And when I would get overwhelmed by the very scary nature of parenting, I would sit quietly with myself (which is actually pretty easy when your child is still in your womb and you live alone) and go over worst-case scenarios. *What if my child had health difficulties? What if I was unable to bond with her? What if my body couldn't produce milk and I couldn't afford formula? What if I lost my job and we had nowhere to live? What if...* a million other scenarios.

I let myself feel these feelings. I allowed the negative thoughts to visit momentarily. It was okay to hear them out. And when the darkness was all aired out, I'd always come back to the same simple conclusion—just feed her and keep her safe. That's it. Wake up each day, or 2 a.m. feeding, and just do those two things, moment by moment. The rest would find its way to me, to us, to our lives and relationship with each other. And neither thing was easy—but I knew, even back then at age 24, that I could do hard things. And keeping my child alive was the bare minimum. I could do it. Everything else would be a bonus.

I didn't know it at the time but I was reframing my anxiety into something a little less scary. I was able to break down the millions of fears and "what ifs" into a simplified version of what it means to be a parent to houseplants, pets, and actual human beings. And what I learned was that it wasn't as hard as I anticipated it would be. It wasn't easy, either. But it was doable. I could do those two things—feeding and keeping alive—and I even had time for things like talking and singing to my baby, and changing diapers. But the point is this: I anticipated the challenges and came up with a plan that worked for me in those moments of overwhelming emotions.

In this exercise, you are going to do the same: anticipate challenges and assign tangible ways to weather them. This type of exercise is not a silver bullet or antidote. It will not guarantee that you always feel positive and capable in pursuit of your Legacy List. But it will give you permission to face challenges, to let those obstacles make you feel some kind of way, and to move forward from there.

You can do this—this specific exercise to create a Legacy List and commit to living an aligned life. You can do all of it.

Time to Write It Down

Let's brainstorm what to do on the hard days.

1. Take a look at each of the six-month priorities from Chapter 6 that you listed for yourself. On a piece of paper or in your digital notes, rewrite each of those priorities, with space below each.

2. Start with that top priority and ask yourself: *What could go wrong? What could make me feel inadequate? Who or what could get in my way?* Free-journal answers to these questions. From there, write a statement reframing that challenge to be less scary and overwhelming.

The following are some examples, drawn from the example goals listed in Chapter 6.

Legacy List Goal: Improve awareness and change treatment for the better for Alzheimer's disease and other forms of dementia.

Six-Month Goal: Continue to educate myself on this cause, including 20 minutes of research or reading about it every day.

Potential Challenges: Time is a huge constraint. Caring for my children at home, and caring for my parent who is struggling with Alzheimer's disease, takes a lot of time in addition to my job and other commitments. Another challenge is knowing what information is the most important and can be trusted on this topic.

Reframe: I need to remember that even five minutes dedicated to improving my knowledge base on this topic helps. I can also split up the time I need to research and read about Alzheimer's disease throughout the day if 20 minutes is just not feasible. Just two minutes per day is an hour per month, which is an hour more than I'd have done otherwise. I can also use this time to find trusted websites and influencers in this space where I can go to find information and content.

Six-Month Goal: Create a list of people I know who can help me reach this goal and either meet with them in person, or create an email or text that explains why I'm investing my time in this cause and how I hope they can help me.

Potential Challenges: People may freeze up at the thought of adding something to their to-do list, or simply skim over my email, texts, or social media content because they are too busy.

Reframe: Even one person who supports me in this cause is valuable. I don't need a response or commitment from everyone I'm contacting or reaching. A small but trustworthy army of helpers can do so much to enact positive change. I should also remember that sometimes people internalize what they read and see, even if they don't act in the moment. By planting this seed in their conscious, I could be creating positive changemakers of the future.

Six-Month Goal: Develop a strategic plan to get my community more involved with my cause. This will include event, networking, and fundraising ideas.

Potential Challenges: Hearing the word "no" when it comes to connecting, securing venues, or asking other people to pitch in.

Reframe: Respect the answers I receive with grace. I would want someone to treat me the same way. It's also valuable to remember that a "no" right now might not be a "no" forever. Simply reaching out shows that I respect that person or organization enough to want to include them in this important cause.

Let's toggle to a different example from Chapter 6's exercise.

Legacy List Goal: Become financially independent and leave no debt to my family.

Six-Month Goal: Speak with an accountant or wealth manager to start my savings plan.

Potential Challenges: Finding the time to commit to this initial meeting and then being willing to heed this expert's advice.

Reframe: The first thing I need to do is make the appointment and show up. I can ask the expert to give me specific steps to take to improve my savings plan and then take those steps before my follow-up appointment.

Six-Month Goal: Enact the advice received on saving money, whether that is a separate account or simply saving more each time I'm paid.

Potential Challenges: Unexpected expenses could arise. There will also be times when I really want to spend money, instead of sticking to my financial plan.

Reframe: It's important for me to stick to my goals as much as possible so when unexpected expenses arise, it is an exception. I will also have the rule that before I can spend money on anything outside of my savings plan, I will reread my Legacy List and decide if that spending item is still worth it.

Six-Month Goal: Pick one thing to stop spending money on each week or month, and then consistently stick with it.

Potential Challenges: My lifestyle will change when I commit to spending less money on things outside my budget or savings plan. This may mean less social outings or spending less on eating or drinking out. I may feel left out or experience low emotions when I make these changes.

Reframe: I need to remember that all change is hard. This is my brain's way of fighting back against things that are unfamiliar. I need to remind myself that feeling left out, or low, does not mean I am doing anything detrimental. Giving up short-term gratification in exchange for long-term stability is preferable, and I'll be thankful later.

And here's a final example from Chapter 6:

Legacy List Goal: Be an even more invested parent or grandparent.

Six-Month Goal: Have at least one meaningful, five-minute conversation with each of my kids each day.

Potential Challenges: Finding five minutes of time each day, distraction-free, to speak with each of my kids. There may also be days my kids are simply not interested in talking to me when I want or have the time to talk to them.

Reframe: Effort speaks volumes. I need to make the concerted effort to reach out to them every day and show interest in what they have going on.

Six-Month Goal: Take an active role in the activities my kids are participating in by volunteering in a small way for one item each.

Potential Challenges: Finding volunteer opportunities that fit into my schedule and allow me to be with my kids in the process. Finding motivation to follow through with these items.

Reframe: Ask my kids directly what activities they'd like me to do more and if they know what other parents do to volunteer. I can also be clear in my time constraints and boundaries when I offer to volunteer so that I find an opportunity that truly fits what I'm able to do.

Six-Month Goal: Actively look for positive feedback for each of my kids.

Potential Challenges: Looking for new ways to encourage them that are authentic and specific.

Reframe: Take the first step by making the effort and understanding that some comments or positive feedback may mean more to them than others. Simply looking for that positivity will encourage them and make a difference.

You cannot predict every challenge, of course, but reframing is great practice for when unexpected bumps in the road pop up.

Conclusion

WHAT'S STILL UNFINISHED?

You've made it through the proverbial obstacle course that is this book—and for that, I congratulate you. You've taken the time and steps to begin building an aligned, purposeful life that will reverberate long after your time here. You've navigated the intricate landscape of your life, unearthing the core of your being and meticulously crafting the blueprint of your Legacy List. This isn't merely a document, it's a testament to your unwavering commitment to a life lived with purpose and intention. The conscious effort you've poured into these exercises, from identifying your deepest values to strategizing for inevitable challenges, lays the groundwork for a future where your influence extends far beyond your immediate presence.

The act of starting, of putting pen to paper or thought to action, is a powerful declaration. It sets in motion a ripple effect that will touch lives in ways you might not foresee, creating connections and inspiring change long after the initial impulse. Trust in the process, and know that your willingness to begin is, in itself, a profound act of legacy building.

As you move forward, remember that the path to building your legacy is not static. It's a dynamic, evolving journey. The tools and insights gained from this book are not just for mapping out your goals, they are for cultivating a heightened, dynamic state of being. By living consistently in alignment with your calling, you will create a cascade of positive influence that stretches far beyond your current horizon. Thank you for answering that call, for daring to live a life that will outlive you, and for making the world a brighter place through your intentional journey.

You've stuck with me for a lot of my personal stories, and I hope that they've made you feel seen, or at least not alone. But like any good storyteller, I'm going to leave you with one more story for the road. I'm proud of you. I know you can do whatever your heart sets out to do.

One More Story

Not long after my mom was diagnosed with early-onset Alzheimer's disease, I received a perspective-changing email from my dad. I was deep in my own grief, and trying to help as much as I could from afar with my mom's care and next steps. My dad and I had been communicating regularly through text, email, and phone calls about all of that, and though the circumstances weren't ideal, it was nice getting to talk to my dad so much.

My mom was usually the one who initiated the phone calls, copied him on emails to me, or handwrote the addresses on the birthday cards they both signed for my kids and me. Now he was tasked with those things, or at least his own version of them. He was also my main source of information about Mom's condition, and I checked in almost daily in those early days for updates.

So I was not surprised to see an email from him in my inbox. The email was short and to the point. Dad had been going through files on the desktop computer he shared with my mom for years, when he came across some works in progress of hers. He had downloaded them in their draft state and attached them to the email for me.

One was a memoir—which she and I had discussed my help with a few years' prior—of her time working with incarcerated youth who were in the Indiana Department of Corrections. She had spent time as both a counselor and a drill sergeant. She had retired early when budget cuts at the state level caused her counseling caseload to triple. She no longer felt safe or able to do her job in the capacity that she wanted. “I’m just a paper pusher now,” she told me once, disappointed that she could not work in the way she knew she was capable.

Upon her early retirement, my mom set to work writing down her experiences and how her time there had influenced her views on the criminal justice system in America. I’d read parts of the work before my dad sent it to me, but had forgotten about it in the chaos that eventually led to Mom’s early-onset Alzheimer’s diagnosis.

Seeing the document in my email wounded me. Here was a document that I had offered to help my mom complete—had every intention of helping her complete, when we both had the time—and it was unfinished. As I read and reread her words, I was moved at the way she wrote with such clarity and compassion. She recounted experiences so perfectly and with such moving details. Sitting there reading those words that I knew flowed from a former version of my mom’s mind, I started to feel overwhelmed with grief. It was like I was reading something from a person I used to know. It was a reminder of the person my mom had been, not very long ago.

The other document was one more personal in nature and one that I’ve yet to finish reading. I keep coming back to it, every few months, and reading more. I can only process pieces at a time.

This other document was not one that I'd known about before this email from my dad. It was a personal journal of sorts, except the writing itself spanned just about a year or so. At some point, just a few years before her Alzheimer's diagnosis, my mom had started writing down as many memories as she could of her life, her children, her grandchildren and her 40-plus-year marriage to my dad. As I read through the memories, I felt grateful to have so many details written down, but felt another pang of yearning: *What memories hadn't made it yet to the unfinished document? What other things had she wanted to add before she was unable to do so? What stories were untold?*

Suddenly every part of my being ached to go back five years and jump into these documents with her, to give her feedback and pull even more memories and insight from her wealth of experience as a counselor, spouse, mother, grandmother, and human being. Her writing was so good, so detailed, so easy to follow. *What would finished manuscripts have looked like? What was still missing? Why hadn't I done more to get these across the finish line?*

Her writings were a true, unexpected gift to receive. But they would never be finished, at least not in the way she would have wanted them to look and read. Her contribution to them was complete, even if the documents were not.

It wasn't a far leap to start thinking about what was still unfinished in my life. I asked myself, *What is unwritten? What are the stories and points of view that only I can tell? How do I ensure that I'm doing all I can to finish as much as possible? Heck. What are the things I haven't even started?*

I felt badly that Mom didn't get to all the things she was working on—the unfinished manuscripts, the writing she started listing memories of my brothers and me, and even the grandchildren she would never get to know. Naturally, it made me reflect on my own lists of unfinished things.

Hello—the whole point of this book.

But as I've faced my grief in the years that have followed, I've started to realize that *just getting started is a huge step in the right direction.* My mom started to write because she had something on her heart—something she wanted to leave behind. And every word on the page is a testament to her legacy building. Without the start of those manuscripts, I wouldn't know the thoughts contained there. I would never know the most-important memories of raising my brothers and me that she just *had* to recount on paper, in hopes that we would read her thoughts about them one day. I would never know the true depths of her compassion for young people who had the decks stacked against them—or realize my responsibility to these young people, too. Even unfinished, the words changed me for the better.

So thank goodness she started them.

And if there is anything I would leave you at the end of this journey we've embarked together, it is this: Starting from an aligned place will get you far. It may not always get you to the ending you imagined, or even the ending at all. But the world will be a better place now and well into the future because you started.

Legacy Building—a Long Game

Legacy building is a long game. The seeds you plant in this life may not bloom fully until after you are gone, after your children or nieces and nephews are gone, after their children are gone from this earth.

Legacy does not have to be world-changing. Legacy starts with one step, one conversation, one moment when you step out of your comfort zone, one new person you meet. The exercises in this book are designed to help you map out the steps to that legacy you are supposed to leave behind. But in doing those actions, you are also more aware of what that legacy path looks like. And by living consistently in that space, you will make a bigger ripple in the greater lake of life—so much so that the ripples will go every direction, and beyond the horizon that you can see. But it starts with knowing who you are and what your ripple is supposed to do.

I hope you are ready to dive into the actions that create a life that will outlive you. Thank you for heeding your calling and making my world a better place in the process.

ACKNOWLEDGMENTS

There are so many people who helped encourage me to get my *Legacy List* process on paper to share with the world—and so many who lent their expertise to make it happen.

First, I want to thank Dr. Lauren Hodges for connecting me with the team at Sound Wisdom Publishing and putting in a good word for me. Read her book *Less Stress, More Calm*. She's brilliant.

I'd also like to thank John Martin and the team at Sound Wisdom for their kindness, patience, and expert eye to make this book look and sound great.

A huge thanks to my team at Space Coast Performing Arts for helping me live out my *Legacy List* through their enthusiasm, expertise, and kindness. Special thanks to Ashley, Brooke, Jeana, and Amy who have been there from the start.

Thank you to my friends who read chapters, helped me process my feelings about some of the things I wrote, and looked over book cover designs. Koren, Pam, Colleen, Virginia, and Dani: I'm especially grateful for you. A big thank you to Rylie for sparking that dandelion idea you see on the book cover.

Thank you to my dad for being an example of what a lifetime of love looks like in action. Your commitment and love for my mom inspires me to give more to all of the wonderful people in my life.

To my mom: I love you. I heard your voice in my head telling me to be brave as I wrote this book. You would love how it turned out.

To my extended family, including my wonderful in-laws, Roger and Maureen, thank you for caring about me and giving me that bonus support when I need it.

And to my husband, Brant, and our five children—Ferris, Emilia, London, Erinn and Teagan—thank you for letting me be "me," even when I'm busy, messy, or cringey. You are truly the best part of this life.

ABOUT KATIE PARSONS

Katie Parsons is a writer, editor, podcaster, and musical-theatre performer, living on Florida's Space Coast with her husband, five children, and three dogs. She spent much of her children's early years as a freelance journalist and is the creator of the blog *Mumbling Mommy.*

Since the spring of 2024, Katie has been at the helm of Space Coast Performing Arts—a studio that offers musical theatre-focused classes, private lessons, summer camps, and productions. Alongside a team of talented teachers and performers, SCPA offers opportunities for performers of all ages, experience levels, and abilities.

Katie is the co-producer and co-host of *Generation In-Between: A Xennial Podcast* where she and her friend Dani talk about pop culture moments from being "1980s kids and 1990s teens."

Her second book, *Next Generation Alzheimer's: Can We Reverse Our Inevitable?,* is in production.

Follow Katie on social media **@bykatieparsons**

Read more from Katie Parsons, book her for speaking engagements or send her your feedback at **ByKatieParsons.com.**

THANK YOU FOR READING THIS BOOK!

If you found any of the information helpful, please take a few minutes and leave a review on the bookselling platform of your choice.

BONUS GIFT!

Don't forget to sign up to try our newsletter and grab your free personal development ebook here:

soundwisdom.com/classics